Taking Care of Me

The Habits of Happiness

by Mary Kay Mueller and *You*!

www.marykaymueller.com

ISBN 0-9654372-2-1

Library of Congress Catalog Card Number: 2002107584

Edited by Tony Mitton
Layout by Pam Bochel
Front cover design by Dale Vermeer
Author's photograph by Andrew Baran

Published by
Insight Inc.

Insight Inc.
P.O. Box 6470
Omaha, NE 68105

Tel: 1-800-419-0444
Email: mkmotiv8@aol.com
www.marykaymueller.com

Contents◄

Dedicated in love
to
 Joanna and Zachary

Preface◀

The turn of the millennium was a big year for me. Changes in offices, publishers, partner, and even my hairdo were external manifestations of internal recreations. I started being okay with being alone. I had a spiritual shift in consciousness. In the midst of it all, someone asked if the book was "all about me."

Yes, I replied. It is all, all about me. And you.

That same year, Sinead O'Connor, the rock/pop/punk artist, also had a spiritual transformation. In her words, "We live under the illusion that we are all separate from each other, and what I believe is that on the soul level, we are one. So if you're honest when you talk about the things you're going through, people feel it. They hear a bit of themselves in there."

That's my intention for this book. That you hear a little bit of yourself and know that we're all on the right path.

So why republish my first book as a workbook? Because of the thousands of readers of *Taking Care of Me: The Habits of Happiness.* It has been your enthusiasm and gratitude for that book that has prompted this one. No more will you have to answer the questions on a separate sheet of paper. This is your book. Write in it. You are writing this story with me. Your words are as important as mine. Thus, the author notation,

by Mary Kay Mueller and <u>You</u>!

Meanwhile, there are some updates. I think they're improvements.

This is also a *playbook.* It could not just be a 'workbook' because anyone who lives a life of taking-care-of-me well knows that it is simply glorious fun. Yet, there is a focus to it, an intention that is like the energy of any work that we love. We do it with a goal in mind — to get us back to playing the game of life. So we work it until it becomes natural and playful again.

▶ WHERE THIS BOOK CAN TAKE YOU

I believe we are each given dreams/maps for our lives along with the keys to a magnificent vehicle. Yet some of us sit in the driveway complaining that no one is getting behind the wheel. Others of us drive off without ever checking the map and often feel lost and directionless.

Still others of us know where we want to go, but keep turning around to listen to the backseat drivers in our lives telling us we're going the wrong way or driving too fast. Yet others forget to refuel our tanks or check the oil, so we spend most of our time broken down by the side of the road.

All of these events have described me at one time or another in recent years. Today, I resolve to be on my way, a way that is uniquely my own, refueling and checking my inner map as I go. This book is to remind us that God is our engine, love is our fuel and joy is our map.

▶ THE TAKING CARE OF ME AUDIO EDITION

For those of you who enjoy long car trips with the tape player going, we offer you an audio version of this material. It is not a verbatim read. Rather it is a live interaction with people on the path to greater happiness much like yourself. If my singing, stumbling and chuckling can enhance your experience, see the last page of this book for details.

▶ ACKNOWLEDGEMENTS

Special thanks to my newest teachers Krissa Lee Regier, Kaylene Smith, John Smith, Sky St. John, Maria Nemeth, Mayla Makena, Abraham-Hicks and Eckhart Tolle. Also, many thanks to my catalysts: writing buddy Ben Forest, and writing support team, Dalene Smith, Phil Grossoehme, Joy Britton, Kerri Drake, Marsha Yentes, Tony Mitton, Thierry and Karin Bogliolo, and Sue Layel.

As always, my deepest thanks to my Jo, Zach and my goombahs, Sarah and Carol. You never ask, "Now what?" You are so good at riding the roller coaster of life with me. Thanks forever and ever. You are the sweetest sweetness in my life!

And finally to You, Loving, Creative Spirit of Life and Source of All That Is, Praise!

InJoy,
Mary Kay

SECTION 1

Introduction◄

We have all heard, "Whatsoever you do to the least of my brethren...."
But what if the least of my brethren is me?

Carl Jung

► THE FIRST DAY OF THE BEST OF MY LIFE

On August 8, 1986, I fled to a domestic violence shelter with my two-year old daughter.

As soon as we arrived, I began to question my right to be there. Most of the other women had broken jaws or cracked ribs. My husband had only knocked me down to prevent me from leaving the house to go to the store. Still, I had told him, "If you do that again, I'll leave you." When it happened again the next day, I realized I had to make an important choice and left.

"Welcome, Mary Kay," the counselor said as she offered me a chair in her small office. Her steady gaze and silver hair were reassuring. "I want to go over some rules with you. One of our counselors will show your daughter to the room where you'll be staying."

A million questions raced through my mind as I nodded and released my little one's hand. "First, do not tell anyone the location of this shelter," the woman continued. "This is a safe haven. You could endanger women's lives."

Again I nodded, trying to let it all sink in.

"The second rule is just as important. For these next four weeks, you may not talk about your husband. You may not so much as mention his name. Do you understand?"

Dumbfounded, I stared at her. "Then what are we going to talk about?"

The naiveté of my question exposed how little I understood about self-esteem and empowerment, subjects I had taught in my high school classroom for years. None of the texts had covered the basic life truths I was about to learn, at age 34, in a women's shelter.

During my month in the shelter, my way of looking at myself and at life altered radically. I realized that living to make others happy was fruitless, that no one can make any one else happy. Therefore, I set out to learn how to be happy myself.

When it came time to leave, the most difficult person to say goodbye to was the silver-haired counselor I had met the first day, whom I had now come to love and trust completely.

"How will I ever be able to thank you for all you've done for me?" I asked through my tears.

"You will share the message," she answered.

And so I have. First, with five neighborhood women in a weekly support group which I called, "Taking Care of Me." Listening to their stories, I knew I was not alone. These women told of giving away their personal power to bosses, spouses, pastors, parents, children and friends. All of us needed to get back in touch with our true selves.

Using what I learned in the shelter and from leading these groups, I developed a program that improved every aspect of my life: my mental and physical health, income, relationships, and spirituality. Today I have shared what I've learned with hundreds of thousands of men and women in corporations, hospitals, schools, churches and shelters throughout the country. It is my great joy to be sharing it now with you.

As we begin our journey together, ask yourself,

What changes would I like to see in my life?

(Take all the time and space you need here. You will come back to this page regularly.)

_____

_____

_____

_____

_____

_____

_____

_____

_____

_____

_____

_____

_____

_____

This workbook can only benefit you if you are honestly ready to look at your life. Ask yourself,

Where could I be more honest with myself? With others?

_____

_____

_____

_____

_____

_____

_____

_____

_____

_____

_____

_____

_____

Wherever you go you will find people lying to you,
and as your awareness grows, you will notice that you also lie to yourself.
Don Miguel Ruiz

▶ THE COURAGE TO BEGIN

Congratulations on beginning! Investing in yourself by reading this book is a very healthy step! Now ask yourself: What kind of person tends to go to a gym regularly? Someone healthy or sick? And what kind of person goes to a worship service regularly? One with stronger or weaker faith?

Obviously, those who are healthier or more faith-full are those who are investing in themselves. We all have "gratitude muscles" and "hope-muscles" that need to be exercised and strengthened by regular workouts. Keeping our gratitude and hope muscles in shape makes good sense. Reading this book will provide you with a format to help discipline yourself in these areas. And those of you who stop and do the exercises will benefit 10 times more from this material than if you just skim through reading it.

Remember, knowing that you can change your life is a sign of high self-esteem and the absolute means to greater happiness. You are on a path that works!

Things do not change. We change.
                              Henry David Thoreau

1. What qualities or behaviors have I strengthened in myself by investing in a process or regular practice? (e.g. wearing a seatbelt, learning a computer program, improving my golf score, etc.)

_____

_____

_____

_____

_____

_____

_____

_____

_____

2. What helped these qualities or behaviors stick? (e.g. the seat belt light, working with a golf pro, etc.)

_____

_____

_____

_____

_____

_____

_____

_____

_____

WHO THIS BOOK IS FOR

I have found this material helpful to anyone who wants to be happier. Most people who pick up this book take better care of others than they do of themselves. There is a chapter at the end of the book on self-nurturing, but the fact is that you already know how to put your feet up and pour yourself some lemonade. It's other issues, like giving yourself permission to do it, that we need to address first.

I do guarantee you that these principals work, and already are at work in your life whether or not you acknowledge them and cooperate with them. You are moving toward greater happiness. This material will simply speed up the process and explain to you why things are happening as they are. Relax and rejoice! You are about to learn how to feel good and maintain a high level of happiness *no matter what!*

 ## GETTING SUPPORTED

The longer I do the work/play of conscious living and joy creation, the more I am convinced that it is much easier and more fun to do this work with others. You may benefit from coaches, teammates, cheerleaders or fans. I have used and continue to use all of these.

▶ Coaches:

A Coach is someone who, at first, empowers us by pulling us out of our old patterns. With a Coach, we learn to trust a new guidance system. They encourage us to do things we would otherwise not do; things we believe we cannot do. At first, this can be frightening. If you are as co-dependent as I was, you are always looking for everyone else to tell you what to do, and if one person's advice didn't suit you, you simply looked elsewhere. With a Coach we learn discipline, first to follow their lead, then to follow our own inner wisdom. Coaches can also be identified by distinct intentions, commitments, and tone:

1. **Intentions**

    Most of us can remember a time when we had an intense yearning for someone to love us, to approve of us, to rescue us. When we get on this tailspin we lose weight, or rearrange our schedules, or have sex, or work 80 hours a week, or spend more on clothes, or all of the above! We allow anyone and everyone who seems like they might fulfill our unfillable need to tell us what to wear, how to act, who to talk to and what to do. Usually our trainer/targets are as unhealthy as we are, and without any strong spiritual connection to sustain them.

    When we look for a Coach, our intention is quite different. We want to get into shape. If our Coach becomes our friend, that is wonderful, but it is not the goal of this interaction. We ask someone to be our Coach because we see that their life is peaceful and happy, and trust them to remind us to go within to find our own peace.

2. **Commitments**

    In a coaching situation both parties make an agreement. The Coach agrees to be there for us on a weekly, monthly, or yearly basis, to guide us. They share their clarity of vision, their steadfastness. They are invaluable because they have played the game themselves and have information that can unlock the mysteries surrounding our stumbling blocks. They are unwilling to be manipulated to get our approval and they model for us how to do likewise.

Meanwhile, Coaches call us to commit, to make promises, and then they hold us accountable. Their main concern is not to make us feel good, but to move us to a new level on the playing field of life. They know that movement takes discipline and perseverance, and that once achieved, will bring us a feel good that will last a lifetime.

3. **Tone**

    The tenor of our communications is not as a rule overly emotional. Our Coaches respect and believe in us and will not allow us to transfer our power onto them. They allow disagreement, even open defiance, and do not get angry when we don't follow their suggestions, for they know that time and pain will move us in the right direction eventually.

    In my life my favorite coaches have been tougher than nails. Nothing I could say would make them change their love for me or their version of the truth. They allowed me to cry without needing to cry with me. As our relationship progressed, they laughed with me as we shared stories of just how interesting our past choices had been.

*Lots of people want to ride with you in the limo,
but what you want is someone who will take the bus with you
when the limo breaks down.*

Oprah Winfrey

How to find/engage a Coach: There are basically two ways to find a Coach. You may hire someone: a counselor or therapist, a weight loss Coach from a reputable program, an executive Coach, etc., who will charge you a set fee in return for regular coaching. Their meetings with you are usually once a week for the first year or so of your transition period, after which they can often be less.

The second kind of Coach is someone who has a program or belief system that you agree to live by. They will help you, on the understanding that as you become stronger on your path, you will turn and coach the next person in need. 12-step programs are the best known form of such coaching, but there are many other mentoring relationships, with or without formalized programs, that can fulfill this need.

Together you and your Coach agree on set goals and a regular check in time. If progress toward the goal is not achieved at the expected rate, a Coach may change the strategy. It is our job to follow their lead. Trust in your Coach must be unequivocal. When you stop trusting them, you need to formally end the coaching agreement as soon as possible and redefine your relationship with them as friend, teammate, etc.

Today I have two coaches I meet with every other week: a financial Coach and a body work-therapist Coach who helps me balance physically, emotionally and spiritually. Sometimes one of them will send me to another Coach for awhile to do some specialized work. Whether you call your Coach a therapist, a sponsor, a mentor, a grandparent or a minister is not important. Trusting your Coach to guide you and moving out of your old patterns could mean the difference between a touchdown and a fumble.

How I envision my perfect Coach:

_____

_____

_____

_____

_____

_____

_____

_____

_____

_____

▶ Teammates:

Sometimes it takes awhile to find just the right Coach. In the meantime, your teammates are your most powerful allies for long-lasting life change. A teammate never costs money. This resource requires only your time. They are companions on the journey, there to listen and learn with us. They don't share advice as much as their own stories of terror and triumph. They could be your sports team, your support group, your book discussion club, or your girl's or guy's night out gang. Every church, every gym and every community has such groups in place. You may decide to join an existing group or to create your own.

"But I don't know how!" I hear regularly from individuals in large and small communities. That's why God invented telephones, paper and the internet! I have begun over a dozen small groups so far, moving friendships or those with similar needs and interests into a more solidified gathering. Every time I did, an important need was met for myself as well as for others.

How to find/engage Teammates: My first experience with a support group began when I realized that I needed a weekly "booster shot" after leaving the shelter. I put notes in eight mailboxes in my neighborhood and five women, three of whom I had never met, showed up at my door the following Saturday morning for the first "Taking Care of Me" group. We met once a week for two years, at which time the group evolved into a class.

I started another group, years later, by inviting 10 friends over two days after Christmas for hot chocolate. When the conversation began to lull, I invited each person to share one thing they had learned from the previous year or their goal for the coming year. Four hours (and three boxes of tissues) later, we decided to form a women's group. The group went through some changes, eventually settling into a group of six of us. We met for three years. It was marvelous.

One of the groups I am involved with today focuses on business and financial goals. Another meets weekly to encourage goal setting and deliberate creation in all areas. A third group consists of those of us who are beginning composers. We meet monthly. It is amazing to me that I can always make time for these get-togethers if I choose to. What is even more amazing is the positive impact they have had on my life.

Each group I have formed or been a part of has agreed upon guidelines to set the tone of our gatherings. Here are some examples:

1. We will own responsibility for our actions and feelings rather than blame other people or circumstances.

2. We will not offer advice except on the rare occasion when it is requested.

3. We will refrain from labels or putdowns of ourselves and others, such as saying that someone is 'stupid'.

4. We will laugh at ourselves, but not at the expense of others or to distract us from our topic.

5. We will focus on the here and now, releasing the concerns of those not in the room and our own regrets about what didn't happen in the past.

6. Each person will get a chance to share at each meeting, an opportunity they may use or pass.

7. Leadership will rotate, as each person holds special gifts to be shared.

8. We will keep all sharing completely confidential.

▶ BENEFITS OF SUPPORT GROUPS

What are the advantages of meeting in small groups?

*   A feeling of normalcy. As you hear the stories of others, you know you are not alone.
*   A safe haven where you know that nothing you can say will dampen the flow of unconditional acceptance from the group.
*   The freedom to be completely honest about whatever is happening in your life.
*   Enhanced progress. As you hear the same issues come up time and again (and they will) you will learn your lessons more quickly.

The support group is not intended to be a gripe session about how awful or strange 'they' are. The more a group separates us from – rather than invites us into – unconditional acceptance of the larger human family, the less healthy it is. You know you've outgrown a group when you use it to share 'top this' stories, when you find yourself repeating something you've shared before, or when you are attending the meetings for 'them'.

Support groups are simply a boat to get us to the other side of the lake.
When we get there we start using our stories for attention, pity, or power.
At this point, it's time to get out of the boat.

Caroline Myss

Author Bernie Siegel, M.D., once wrote that if everyone had a one-hour group to meet with each week where they could be completely honest, there would be no physical or mental illness on the planet. I believe him.

Jot down some thoughts on support groups:

Am I interested in joining one that's already existing? Am I willing to start one, knowing that attendance may be as small as 2 or 3 people for the first few months?

_____

_____

_____

_____

_____

_____

_____

_____

▶ Cheerleaders and Fans:

These folks are on our sidelines. They are the people we can pick up the phone and call, or e-mail or visit at the drop of a hat. They have no way of knowing all the daily ups and downs of our journey, nor do they need to. They may never have dealt with our issues. Although they cannot understand everything we're describing, they believe in us. They don't care about the scoreboard. They are there with that "It's so good to hear from you" uplift that reminds us that we are bigger than any event or circumstance. They call us back into the NOW of presence with their unconditional love.

Also, when need be, they invite us to play and lighten up. This is not a distraction from our program, it is a time to breathe and recharge. Cheerleaders don't ask a lot of probing questions. They want only the best for us. They are there with a hug between games to remind us that life is more than learning new plays and racking up points.

How to find/engage Cheerleaders and Fans: Look to those around you. Friends and family who have been there for you in the past are usually just waiting in the bleachers to be called into service.

One of my girlfriends gave me the key to her home during the days when I just needed a quiet get-away. That symbol of her trust and love for me was a huge comfort in one of my most challenging times.

Today my walking partners are cheerleaders for me. I know that if I want to go to a movie or need someone to pick up a child from school, they will be there. I have two wonderful friends and a wonderful Mom who send me cards at just the right times to say they're praying for me or thinking of me. I also have an e-mail buddy who gets my overflow of emotions from time to time. She just listens and acknowledges the wonderful path that I am on. It is a marvelous gift.

As you look over these descriptions, make a note of:

• which kinds of support systems you have relied on in the past
• why they were helpful or less than helpful
• which are active in your life right now
• which you would like to add to your game plan

_____

_____

_____

_____

_____

_____

_____

_____

No matter how you plan to use this material, or what support systems you invite in for the journey, know that your strong, clear intention to succeed is the most important component. Therefore, do not judge yourself during this process, but use this text to track your progress along your journey. You will be amazed how quickly results will come.

▶ THE HAPPINESS BARGAIN

Consider all the facets of your life for a moment: physical, emotional, spiritual, financial, mental, relational, etc. If you traded in whatever percentage of your life isn't "working" right now, knowing that it would improve, what percentage would you be trading? 5%? 25%? 75%? 95%?

_____

_____

All right, here is **The Happiness Bargain:** whatever percentage you traded in of areas where you want to see improvement, that is the percentage of *your belief system* that needs to be changed.

The statistics on women recovering completely from domestic violence, and never again getting into a physically or emotionally abusive relationship with a man are grim. I beat the odds. It was not because I had a higher IQ, was more stubborn or was more scared. I was not the best, the brightest or the boldest at that shelter. It was because I was the blankest!

I walked into that shelter a blank slate, freely admitting I didn't know what the hell I was doing, so I was willing to start from scratch. That's why I'm able to write this book today about a lifestyle that is happier and healthier than I could have imagined.

So, are you ready to open your mind and trade in that "not working" percentage of your belief system for greater peace and joy?

No one ever died from the draft
of an open mind.

Last but far from least: the percentage you kept, the percentage of your life that is working? That is your Score.

On this date: _____

my Score is: _____

My goal by: _____

is to have a Score of: _____

I will be coaching you on how to raise your Score throughout the book. It is my contention that with this material and 30 days of your faithfulness to it, your Score will change dramatically for the better.

A spaceship uses close to 75% of its fuel in take off. These first steps you're taking may seem hard and slow, but they will make your journey easier and smoother.

Your engines are fueled. InJoy your trip!

►Getting a 'Head' Start

People are just about as happy as they make up their minds to be.

Abe Lincoln

► THE PHRASE THAT CHANGED MY LIFE

I could hardly believe what I was hearing from the counselor that first morning in the shelter.

"While you are here, we will talk only about you. He is not the problem. You are. We believe there are no adult victims, only volunteers."

"You're saying I chose this?" I asked.

"In a way, yes."

"Why would anyone run from happiness and choose misery and chaos?" I demanded.

"That's a very good question, Mary Kay. You'll be here for four weeks. You'll have plenty of time to think about it. I'm sure you'll find the answers you're looking for." And so I did.

"No adult victims, only volunteers," initially sounded like the worst possible news. It was actually the best. If I was the problem, I was obviously the solution. Once I accepted that premise, I saw that I could continue to volunteer to live in fear, misery and chaos; or I could volunteer for happiness, health and more loving relationships. I could choose a life of struggle or a life of ease. But to experience real ease I had to experience release; I had to release old beliefs and unlearn old habits. I had to replace them with new, sometimes radically different thoughts.

► THE FUNDAMENTAL BELIEF

In a 10-year study by the National Institute on Aging, it was found that the happiest people in the world had a variety of attributes in common. The most important happiness factor was, "...the belief *that they had the power to take control of their lives.*" This concept of personal responsibility and power became the foundation for my recovery program.

The process of owning our power begins with the realization that we have within us the cure for what ails us. This awareness forces us to go beyond blaming circumstances or people for our predicaments.

> *People are always blaming their circumstances.*
> *I don't believe in circumstances.*
> *People who get on in this world*
> *are the people who get up and look for the circumstances they want,*
> *and if they can't find them, make them.*
>
> George Bernard Shaw

▶ B.C. OR A.D.?

This program invites you to move forever and completely from victim to victor. It is the difference between living in B.C. and A.D.

Unhappy, negative attitude individuals live in **B.C.** — Blaming and Complaining.

"If only he..." "If only she...." "If only they..." thoughts cloud their vision and distract them from their dreams. They give away their power by believing they have none.

Happy, positive attitude individuals live in **A.D.** Whenever something does not go as planned in their lives, they Act to get back on track, and/or Dream and visualize what they want to manifest.

If someone were to ask me why my life is like it is, I would most likely tell them...

_____

_____

_____

_____

_____

_____

How much of the time am I in B.C.?

_____

_____

_____

At first it might seem that buying into the "No Victims" paradigm could bring more pain than we could bear. In an attempt to deny that we can be so powerful, we often throw ourselves into the busy-ness of life so we don't have to think about it. We become one of those whom Thoreau described as living a life of "quiet desperation."

▶ WHEN LIFE TURNS UP THE HEAT

A laboratory experiment done in the '60's brings home this point with painful clarity. Scientists, long before we knew better, put frogs into a pot of hot water, and noted that they jumped out instinctively. Yet, when the same creatures were placed in an open pot of cold water placed on a burner where the heat increase was gradual, a very different response occurred. The uncomfortable frogs 'put up with' the increased heat for too long, and all were boiled to death.

Pain is Required,
Suffering is Optional

It sometimes feels like being stripped naked in a snowstorm to suggest that suffering is optional. The belief that suffering is forced upon us is the key to why it is so painful. If we at any time determined that we could stop suffering, but still continued with it, we'd be fools, and no one likes to see themselves as foolish.

Often, a radical change is required to end the suffering, and because of our resistance to change, it is often painful. (Ask any mother of a 25-year-old who has had to tell her son she's decided not to do his laundry anymore!) Thus, we accept unhappiness and suffering as our lot in life. During my recovery, I realized that this resignation was deadly for me and set out to discover why I had stayed in hot water for so long.

In his book, *Love, Medicine and Miracles,* Dr. Bernie Siegel writes about the perils of suffering silently. He cites research by Dr. William Morton of the University of Oregon which found the cancer rate for housewives was 54% higher than the general population, and 157% higher than women who worked outside the home.

When these results were first published, it was assumed there was a carcinogen
in the kitchen, and much fruitless research was spent looking for it...
However, salaried domestics have less cancer than housewives,
despite working in two kitchens...

Little thought had been given to the possibility that the housewives' high risk of cancer could be due to their feeling trapped. Often, these women expressed feeling "cut off from the fuller life" they wanted because they chose to follow the path that others indicated they *should* be living. Their seemingly small daily suffering cumulatively led to a potentially deadly disease.

Certainly it is not the case that one lifestyle choice is better or worse than another. While the above research may have uncovered some stay-at-home Moms who wanted to work, a 1994 survey of 800 women by author Liz Curtis Higgs discovered that 30% of working women surveyed wanted to stay at home full time.

Definition of Stress:
When your heart is in one place and your body is in another.

When asked to list their daily activities under a *should* or *want* column, most men and women find their lives filled with *shoulds*. These are the same individuals whose stress levels are higher and whose health is poorer than their peers. "But isn't pursuit of happiness selfish?" I am asked repeatedly.

No.

▶ PARENTING AND HAPPINESS

I regularly ask groups of parents what it is they want for their children. "Happiness" is always their reply. I remind them that their children are watching. What they often see are their parents saying, "Honey, I want so much for you to be happy, I'm going to make myself miserable just so you can be happy." Remember, they want to be just like us when they grow up, which will mean they'll be miserable for their kids' sake, who will be miserable for *their* kids' sake, who...

To be unhappy now so that we or someone else will be happy later is a common scenario in modern life. It's one we'll talk about later in the chapter on Habit B, "Be Here Now."

For now, let us simply remind ourselves...

Happiness cannot be put on the lay-away plan.
It's only in the present moment that we can find it.

Speaking to a group of us in health and wellness careers, the noted physician and best selling author Dr. Deepak Chopra addressed the happiness question head-on.

"What is the greatest cause of death in this country?" he asked.

Most of the audience answered, "Heart disease."

"Cardiovascular disease, yes. And what is the greatest cause of cardiovascular disease?"

"Stress," we replied.

"It is unhappiness. If you are happy, you are safe. If you are not, you must go find what gives you joy...The greatest number of heart attacks occur on Monday mornings between the hours of seven and nine, to people driving to jobs they do not enjoy."

Later that evening he asked us, "Why do you in America work so hard?"

We chuckled as a gentleman yelled out, "To have money!"

"And why do you want this money?" Chopra continued.

To which the man's response was, "To buy things!"

" And why do you want to buy things?"

"To be... happier."

"Why not be happy first?" the doctor asked. "Then everything else will follow."

Truly happy individuals are far from selfish. Selfishness is defined as "showing care only for oneself." Take time now to write out the names of 5 of the happiest people you have met. They may be living or have passed on.

_____

_____

_____

_____

_____

Now, take a look at your list. Would you say the happiest people are those who have nothing to give to others?

Hardly. It is the unhappiest among us who believe they are too broken to have anything to give; thus they cut themselves off from life, digging a hole of self-pity so deep they can't see the beauty around them or within them.

In contrast, the happiest among us know they have something to give, and give it, then reap more from the giving, become happier, and continue the cycle.

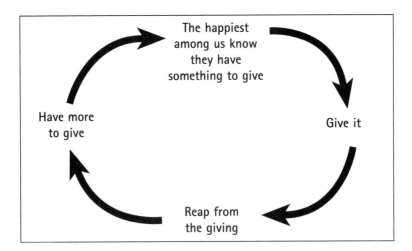

Taking care of our needs through regular self-nurturing must come before nurturing others, not because it is more important, but because we must do first things first. It's not more important to put gas in the car than to drive your kids to school, but if you don't do the first, you may not be able to do the second.

Taking care of yourself and finding personal joy in life is part of every person's life mission. As Stephen Covey, author of *The 7 Habits of Highly Effective People* notes, "We must sharpen the saw before we tackle the woodpile of the day."

Living with the goal of making others happy is as frustrating as it is fruitless. Once I looked back over my adult life. I could see that my acting like a doormat was only training others to wipe their shoes on me. Neither I, nor the person who 'uses' me in this manner, comes away feeling good about it.

The Golden Rule:
Do unto others as you would have them do unto you.
The Silver Rule:
Do for yourself at least as much as you do for others.
The Iron Rule:
Don't do for others what they can do for themselves.

As you become more authentic, follow more of your dreams, ask for what you need, and set limits on your time and energy expenditures, is there a chance that you will lose a couple of friends? Yes, but if they leave your life, did you lose a friend or just an inaccurate assessment?

▶ THE MOST LOVING CHOICE

When I finally understood what the counselor had meant when she said, "No adult victims, only volunteers," I realized that happiness was within my reach. It was also clear that being happy was the most loving thing I could do for those around me. I began my search to learn how to accept life's most wonderful gift.

I soon realized, like Dorothy and her friends in *The Wizard of Oz,* that what I was seeking had always been within me. I just needed to remind myself that the witches and demons could be melted once I exercised my God-given wisdom and power.

▶ THE ATTRACTION FACTOR

I am often asked if "No victims, only volunteers" means we create the negatives in our lives? I prefer to think of it as attracting either negative or positive experiences. When unpleasantness comes our way, we can see it as a reflection of what is inside of us and turn it into a 'trampoline' to bounce up to a new, higher Score. This was made clear to me when I began dating again at age 36.

It was two years after my divorce, and I realized I had very few men friends. I decided, somewhat reluctantly, to join a video dating service. The first time I got a call from the service telling me that I had been selected by a gentleman, I went into their office to see the video of his interview. As I watched, I felt nothing positive or negative, so I went up to the desk and said, "I guess I can meet him for lunch."

At this point, the owner walked over and asked, "Oh, who selected you?" When she saw his name she said, "I don't believe it! Over 500 men and you've attracted the only alcoholic in the service!"

"I didn't attract him! He selected *me*!" I said, trying to defend myself. She simply replied she was not going to allow me to go out with him. She later put a note in his chart saying, "Sometimes Pete drinks too much."

On my next visit to my counselor, I asked her if I had actually attracted the problem drinker. She told me that I could be in a room of 1,000 healthy men and the least healthy one would find me and ask me out. She reminded me that we attract people who are at our same Score. Her good news was that as I learned healthier thinking and feeling habits, I would attract healthier relationships. And so it has been.

So how do we rebound from our lower Score days? *One grateful thought at a time.*

▶ ALLOWING OUR PAIN TO WAKE US UP

On October 29, 1995, the cover story in *Parade* magazine recounted the lessons Captain Scott O'Grady learned after being shot down behind enemy lines in Bosnia. His stories of eating leaves and insects to survive illustrate how he handled living in constant fear and deprivation for six days.

The article heading included this quote: "With death at my front door, I found my key to life." Later in the article, O'Grady said, "I underwent a rebirth... My time in Bosnia was completely positive... I felt the most incredible freedom... I realized I was a spiritual being having a human experience... I knew I'd never be lost again." For years thereafter, Captain O'Grady spoke around the country of his gratitude for the lessons of his experiences. His Score was much higher due to his painful experience.

Every adversity can either make you bitter or better.

In Cherie Carter Scott's book *If Life is a Game, These are the Rules*, her first four Rules for Being Human are:

- *You will receive a body*
- *You will be presented with lessons*
- *There are no mistakes, only lessons*
- *A lesson is repeated until learned.*

The good news is that we do not have to endure extreme or painful conditions to raise our Score. The same outcome can be the result of listening to a grandparent, watching a flower grow, or reading a book. Unfortunately, for those of us too stubborn to believe it until we see it, we must often experience what we don't want in order to move toward what we do.

Once we accept that there are no mistakes, only lessons, we feel more in control of our lives. The shelter was the worst and the best thing that could have ever happened to me. Because it was the worst, I learned my lesson well.

All things work to good...
Romans 8:28

So, is it possible to see that every challenge in our lives has a purpose? To be grateful that everything, everyone, every circumstance can actually work to our good? YES! I vividly recall a conversation with a woman who was on a speaking docket with me. "Do you know why Nelson Mandela [the first black president of South Africa] had to go through being locked up for 27 years? Because behind those bars, with guards all around him, was the only safe place for that man on the planet!"

I was as much amazed at her surety as I was by her insight. I reflected that many indigenous tribes separate their leaders from society before allowing them to take their place at the head of their people. Here was fate handing Mandela a place of safe solitude to prepare him for his destiny. I thought of his incredibly strong belief system that kept him in a positive, grateful frame of mind through the two and a half decades of his confinement.

In order to sustain a positive attitude about our dreams while we are awaiting their fulfillment, we have to believe in a bigger picture than we ourselves can see at the time. I have a few of these in my 'hope' pocket. One of these variations I call the Movie-Maker Mindset.

▶ MOVIE-MAKER MINDSET

Beyond subject matter, scripts and camera angles, there is something inherently spiritual about the genre of film. It is in film that we are given the bird's eye view, the bigger picture of life. We can see, for example, in a *When Harry Met Sally* or *While You Were Sleeping*, how perfectly timed the meetings had to be. We can see in the first *Rocky* or in *Rudy* the makings of greatness, long before anyone but the hero forecasts a happy ending.

As we come to truly understand that thought is creative, film gives us our avenue to salvation. When I drop my purse at the store and everything falls out, I can either feel small and stupid or cute and endearing. Nowadays, when I have such experiences, I simply say (sometimes aloud), "I'm having a Meg Ryan moment." In this way, rather than judging myself, I look through a soft and forgiving camera lens that will eventually tell the story of just how wonderful I am and how this idiosyncrasy of mine is really harmless.

It was film that gave me this reframing perspective, and I can go to my 'movie-maker mindset' anytime I am tempted to judge or despair. *All shall be well.* Even the seemingly terrible moments of life are redeemed as we follow the unfolding of our life's film. We can go back and see the weaving of perfection and the resurrection of the protagonist starting from the film's opening shot. Film reminds us that it is often darkest before the dawn. This is not illusion, this is the truest of truths.

I am right where I need to be today,
this moment.

1. What snags in my life script so far have turned out well in the 'end'?

_____

_____

_____

_____

_____

_____

_____

_____

2. What snags that I am encountering these days could I choose to see differently?

_____

_____

_____

_____

_____

_____

_____

_____

So why do we as movie directors and scriptwriters allow or attract pain? Sometimes we allow painful circumstances to come into our lives because, on some level, we know that what we will gain from the experiences will be worth the pain. Other times, it is just our negative thoughts and feelings *mani-festering* days, weeks or months later. Life teaches lessons through our challenges. Therefore, our job is not to blame others or ourselves, but to continually re-focus on gratitude and joy.

Good Judgment comes from experience.
Experience comes from poor judgment.

▶ SIMPLE, NOT EASY

You have begun the most exciting change of all: becoming more fully who you are. It is the journey of integrity. Throughout this workbook, you will feel yourself being pulled closer and closer to a congruity between what you know to be true and what you live. We either live the truth today or we have to face the truth tomorrow.

As your guide for this part of the journey, I promise that the steps you will learn here are simple but not always easy. If some of these life-changing concepts seem too simplistic, let me return to the wisdom of *The Wizard of Oz.*

When Glinda, The Good Witch, appears to show Dorothy how to go home, she simply shares her heel-tapping instructions with the phrase, "There's no place like home."

Hearing this, the Scarecrow is indignant. "Wait a minute!" he challenges. "If it was that simple, why didn't you tell her before?" Glinda responds with her all-knowing smile, "Because she wouldn't have believed me." We often must walk life's yellow brick road before we understand the simple lessons at the end.

Changing our minds and opening our hearts requires immense honesty and courage. Another of my favorite wizard stories is from the cartoon series by Johnny Hart, creator of *The Wizard of Id* cartoons. In this particular strip, Rodney, the cowardly knight, goes to the Wizard's cellar to request a favor. Rodney explains that he is preparing to go into battle the next day and needs something to make him courageous and strong. The Wizard tells him to have a seat, turns to his cupboard, and pulls out a three-foot hypodermic syringe. When he turns back to the knight, Rodney has run away.

Once we realize that pain is required but suffering is optional, we have new courage to face temporary discomfort for the benefits of a long-term outcome.

▶ THE MOST IMPORTANT QUESTION

As I shared earlier, my final question to the counselor on my first day in the shelter was: "Why would anyone run from happiness and choose misery and chaos?"

We will hear some answers in the next chapter, but before we do, take a moment to imagine this scenario:

Any minute now, a courier is due to arrive at your front door with a beautifully wrapped package containing Abundant Happiness. The package has your name on it.

Why might some people in this situation be tempted to run out the back door?

Turn the page and jot down three or four answers to why people run from happiness, and then put them aside before continuing.

4 Reasons Why People Run from Happiness

_____

_____

_____

_____

_____

_____

_____

_____

Be the change you seek.

Ghandi

The Four Reasons◄
We Run From
Happiness

There is no duty we so underrate as the duty of being happy.

Robert Louis Stevenson

First, let's define happiness. We aren't talking about the kind of feel-good that's 'I-got-what-I-wanted-so-I'll-smile-for-the-next-10-minutes-until-I-want-something-else happiness'. True happiness is not affected by what other people give or don't give us. It's not the absence of all mads or sads, nor is it constantly feeling 'up'. We're talking here about a state of being much larger than any transient emotion. Others have named it joy, peace, serenity, gratitude, bliss. We'll just refer to it as happiness.

My stay at the shelter helped me realize that I had been choosing to run from happiness for most of my life. Now, after listening to the stories of thousands of adults, I realize that most of us unconsciously reject happiness at some point. Why would anyone do such a thing?

Over the past 10 years, I have posed the question to hundreds of groups of varied economic status, ethnicities and ages. Every group has given me the same four responses, usually word for word. Compare your answers with theirs:

Fear of Getting It ①

The Four Reasons We Run From Happiness:

✔ **1. Fear of Getting It**

☐ **2. Fear of Losing It**

☐ **3. The Belief That We Don't Deserve It**

☐ **4. Guilt**

The first fear is also referred to as "fear of change," "fear of the unknown," or "fear of success." Certainly, greater happiness brings change. Will happiness mean we have to change careers or our group of friends? Not necessarily, but if our pursuit of happiness entails such changes, we will want to make them when the time comes.

I'll never forget the gentleman at my first corporate seminar who blurted out, "Hey, if I were really happy, what would I talk about at break?" He feared, as many of us do, that happiness was boring.

▶ Is Happiness Boring?

I remember growing up thinking nice guys were boring, stable jobs were boring, and healthy foods were boring. The concept that happiness and excitement are mutually exclusive is perhaps best promoted by the soap operas, with their dozen new crises each program. Does high excitement = low happiness?

Well, do most people at a casino, the hub of excitement, look happy as they sit at their machines? True happiness does not exclude excitement; it just doesn't depend on it, or on anything else external. Real happiness is an inside job.

I find that the more peaceful and happy I become, the more I am able to release high levels of drama from my experience. I have to put out fewer 'fires' from frenetic living. But there are many more sources of excitement that are not crisis related. For example, my excitement and enthusiasm for the risks of following my dreams has increased.

> *We are never given a dream*
> *without the power to make it come true.*
>
> Richard Bach

Today, knowing I can achieve anything I can conceive, my life is far from dull. Dozens of times in the past few years I have followed my heart, and it has always given me a lot of exciting things to talk about at break!

If I wrote down 10 of my dreams as of this moment, they would include:

_____

_____

_____

_____

_____

_____

_____

_____

_____

_____

▶ DREAMS COMING TRUE

I recall in 1990 wanting an interview with best-selling author Nathaniel Branden in Los Angeles. I had read many of his books, and his tape-set *The Psychology of High Self-Esteem* had changed my life. I wanted to interview him before starting my national speaking tour, so I called him and he most generously agreed to meet with me if I could come out in August of that year.

When I got off the phone I was ecstatic, but I wasn't sure where the $500 airfare to Los Angeles would come from, since most of my income went back into supporting my new business. Nevertheless, I believed I was given this dream, and with it the power to make it come true.

That day, I began talking with friends about how exciting it was going to be to meet him. The next Sunday, after the service where I directed a gospel choir, my pastor asked if I would consider taking a trip. He had heard a wonderful Catholic gospel choir in Los Angeles and wanted me to experience it for myself.

"Of course, the parish will pay your airfare in gratitude for all you have done," he added.

I told him that would be great.

I then called the church in Los Angeles to make sure the St. Brigid's choir was singing on Sundays in August. After the secretary assured me they were, she and I chatted about my trip. Then she asked,

"Would you like to stay in our guest house?"

I told her that would be great.

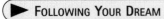

I was able to hear the choir, meet the beautiful people of St.Brigid's, interview one of my all-time heroes, and visit Universal Studios — all in the same weekend. How exciting!

▶ FOLLOWING YOUR DREAM

A friend of mine shared that she had always wanted to move to California, but never seemed to be able to save up enough money to do so. Finally, still with little in her billfold, she set out to follow her dream. She found a job in the area where she wanted to live, but it didn't pay much. One day, as part of her belief that dreams become reality, she got out a sheet of paper and wrote down what it was she wanted to manifest in her life.

Her list was simple: clay to do some sculpting, painter jeans, the kind with the loop on the side, and tennis shoes to replace her heavy hiking boots. Ah, she thought, that would be true happiness. She put away the piece of paper and told noone.

To this day she marvels at the unfolding of events. One week later, a friend who was moving out of town stopped over. "I'm just trying to clean some things out. Why don't you look through this box and see if there's anything you want." She agreed and accepted the closed box.

Shortly after he left, she opened it to find only three items: a ball of clay, painter jeans, and tennis shoes that just fit! No soap opera episode or mystery novel can compare with the excitement of following our dreams.

So why don't we all just do that, follow our dreams?

> *Suffering is what human beings do best.*
> *What takes real courage is to be happy.*
>   Nathaniel Branden

When best-selling author Sid Simon gave a workshop at Creighton University in the late '70's, he referred to a recent study conducted by two psychotherapists. This couple's yearlong sabbatical was spent interviewing the happiest people they could find in 33 different countries.

Their research found that an individual's level of happiness is determined largely by one component: a four-letter word.

What's your guess for the 4 letter word for the key to happiness?

_____

When I speak to women's groups around the world, their common response is 'love'. Yet we know that anyone who is miserable the week before walking down the aisle will be miserable the year after walking down the aisle. Rings on fingers do not happiness make, or we would not have a 53% divorce rate.

When I ask primarily male audiences, I hear anything from 'golf' to 'cash'. But again, we can look to those who win the lottery. If the day before winning they are miserable, one year later...

> *Our co-worker was never really all that happy,*
> *but when she won the lottery, her life just fell apart.*
> Patty, Des Moines, Iowa

We are not trying to put the blame here on money, for those who are happy the day before winning the lottery have been shown to be happy in the ensuing years. It goes back to the difference between a short-term high, which winning obviously would be, and long-term joy. If you need the money to make you happy, then you won't be happy once you've won it.

What about 'time' as the four-letter word? Surely if we all just had more time, everything would be better. Again, what of the young co-worker who won the lottery? Certainly she had more time on her hands, yet had not found happiness. The glaring truth, which we will discuss more deeply later, is that we busy ourselves in order to run from the very happiness we crave.

Families invite the soccer monster to invade their together time every weekend. Couples welcome the cable monster to invade their intimacy time every evening. Neither of these were around just two generations ago. We created them, then fed them until they grew so large they took over our lives. Neither soccer nor TV has the power to give us happiness, nor do they have the power to take it away. For some people, having more time is just having more time to be miserable.

The therapists who did the worldwide study found that the four-letter word is not something that can be bought or won. It is nothing that occurs outside ourselves. The four-letter word for the key to happiness they discovered was <u>risk</u>. Love and joy, peace and prosperity come to those who risk.

The greatest happiness begins at the edge of our comfort zone.

What makes a risk taker special? They trust life and they trust themselves. Risk-takers do not second-guess themselves with "What if?" questions. They live life from the inside out, giving little thought to what others think or say. They may not achieve instant popularity, but they know the supreme happiness of unshakeable integrity.

But how do we get to a point where we care less about what others think?

In 1994, the top box-office hit up to that time was a gentle movie about a gentle man. What endeared *Forrest Gump* to our hearts is discussed more in my book, *God Goes To Hollywood: A Movie Guide for the Modern Mystic*, but to me the key to his endearing qualities was his ability to be a moment to moment risk-taker.

One of my favorite scenes shows Forrest running across the country because he 'feels like it'. At first dismissed as crazy, he is soon lauded as a folk-hero, and hundreds of people decide to run with him. Then one day, he stops and goes home, leaving his stunned followers to find their own path.

> *A new idea is first condemned as ridiculous*
> *and then dismissed as trivial, until finally*
> *it becomes what everybody knows.*
>
> William James

▶ THE GREATEST RISK

Working with a group of GED students one afternoon, I was asked, "If taking risks is so important, what kinds of risks are we supposed to take?" Grateful for the young woman's question, I put it back to her.

"What is the greatest risk you could take between now and the day you die?"

Your answer:

_____

_____

_____

_____

With a hushed voice, she answered, "To be myself." Her answer is true for all of us.

Forrest Gump was a huge box-office draw for a world needing to be reminded of the importance of being ourselves and speaking our truth. As I looked back over my pre-shelter days, I realized that I had spent my life trying desperately to please my parents, bosses, students, church, boyfriends, and eventually, my husband. Nowhere had I truly succeeded.

There were occasional compliments and awards, but even they could not make me happy. I had become a chameleon, changing my exterior behaviors and appearance to get 'love' from others. Therefore, since no one had ever seen the *real* me, when people complimented me, I concluded that they were merely complimenting the aspect of me I had created to please them.

When I accepted my painful failure to make others happy, I released a huge amount of guilt and fear. As I began to be more self-comfortable and authentic, I got to know new levels of joy and love. First, I experienced greater self-love. I began to embrace myself with all my strengths and shortcomings. Then came a new level of acceptance from those who celebrated the real/new me. The friends I kept, after putting them through the 'fire' of my new selfhood, turned to gold.

Today I look at my life and my wonderful friendships and am extremely grateful. We acknowledge each other's imperfections, but we accept and love each other 'in spite of' rather than 'because of....' We are candid and straight with each other. When things go awry between us, we pick up the phone or get together and talk about it, usually the same day. In short, we take huge risks to be who we really are. We are drawn to each other because we are all risk-takers.

1. 3–5 risks I'm glad I've taken ...

_____

_____

_____

_____

_____

2. 3–5 risks I'd like to take but haven't yet...

_____

_____

_____

_____

_____

3. What has kept me from taking each of these risks...

_____

_____

_____

_____

_____

Note: If you had any trouble completing question 2, turn to page 40 and read over our 101 Risks list. It may spark a desire in you.

If you wrote down anything about fear for question 3, you're not alone. Almost everyone who honestly assesses their hesitation to risk has to acknowledge this factor in their decisions.

Fear of Getting It

► FEAR

My favorite acronyms for **FEAR** is: False Evidence Appearing Real. *Our* fear always feels the 'most real' and 'the biggest', yet ask yourself this:

Q: Who has more fear, a coward or a hero? (Or do they both have the same amount?)

When you think about it, it's clear that both the times we backed down from taking a risk, and the times we pushed forward to take it, were fear-full experiences. The difference is that when we hesitate, we use the fear as an excuse to stay stuck, while when we are heroic, we feel the fear and do it anyway. The hero's mindset is one of "What have I got to lose?"

In the big picture, there is no such thing as loss, simply transformation. What we have to gain from risk varies, depending on which of the three categories the risk falls into: Public, Personal, or Private.

► PUBLIC RISKS

What does a public risk look like? These are the times we stand up to others for what we believe. Some examples of public risks in my own life include:

*   Writing a letter to the editor of my university newspaper about the lack of a campus ministry center. The day after the paper came out, I received a phone call from the university president with an offer to let me select a campus ministry house out of four they owned that were in the process of renovation.

*   Adding a drummer, a bass player, and a sax player to our Catholic church choir long before others in our area had done so. Within two years it quadrupled the attendance at that liturgy.

*   At a town hall meeting, interrupting a gentleman who was rattling on about "bombing the Commies," with, "Excuse me, but have you ever met a Russian citizen?" I doubt that it changed his mind, but he did end his diatribe.

There are a number of the public risks I've taken that did not go as planned. I remember taking a Sunday choir job at a Presbyterian Church during my college days. It was 'just a job' where I walked in, put on my choir robe, and sang my solo. I didn't even know anyone's name, other than the choir director's.

It was the eighth or ninth such Sunday, and the preacher was slamming his fist on the pulpit as he shouted warnings to us about the hell-fires awaiting sinners. Suddenly, something inside me snapped.

"Pastor," I interrupted, my heart pounding as I stood facing the astonished congregation. "We have heard we are sinners for the past three weeks. We have heard about hell for the past three weeks. When are we going to hear the good news, that we are forgiven and loved?"

At that point, I ran out of the church (leaving the choir robe at the door) never to return again. The pastor called me later that week to thank me for my candor. He said coffee and rolls after church developed into a most "invigorating discussion." But despite his invitation, I never went back. I simply could not face those people again after my judgmental words.

▶ PERSONAL RISKS

Personal risks are the one-on-ones. They include those times you tell a friend that something she said hurt you or that you really appreciate him and haven't ever expressed it. It can also be spiritual or body work, such as massage, rebirthing, or having your aura picture taken. Some personal risks in my life include:

- Asking John Rosemond, author of six books on parenting, if I could be a part of his national team one minute after introducing myself at his seminar. He later offered me a speaking contract.

- Walking up and introducing myself to Senator Bob Kerrey, who had run for President the previous year. I mentioned to him that since it was 12:30 on a Sunday afternoon and he was in his jeans, I could tell he hadn't been to church yet. He smiled and said, "I meant to go." We chatted and he started attending our service a few weeks later.

- Doing a rebirthing session to clear away old relationship issues.

My greatest personal risk was the Thanksgiving Day my family will never forget. I walked up to the television set we were all watching, turned it off , and stood in front of it. "Are we going to talk about the fact that I was in a shelter, or is this one more secret we are going to sweep under the rug and pretend never happened?"

After they recovered from their shock, we began a discussion/debate that concluded with prayers and hugs five hours later.

Q. What would you guess is the most often repeated three word phrase in the New Testament of the Bible?

_____

(Turn to the bottom of the next page for the answer!)

The personal risks I've taken that did not seem to end well are etched in my mind. They have been relatively few in number, very painful, and extremely enlightening. The one I recall most vividly involved my best friends.

At a party in my honor, I introduced my two good friends to each other, knowing they shared many interests. They hit it off immediately. Soon afterwards, they decided to build me a gift for my upcoming wedding. It would be a surprise! The result was that they and their significant others met two nights a week, leaving little time for outings in which I could be included.

When the wedding week arrived, I received their beautiful bookcase with great joy. Since the project was finished, I would now have my friends back! But they continued to make plans without including me or us, and I felt more and more isolated.

One day, about a month after the wedding, one of my friends was walking into choir practice at the same time I was. I asked her if we could speak a moment in private. We slipped into a chapel and sat down. As I began to share with her that I felt like I'd lost my two best friends, the tears began to flow. "I'm sorry," I said as I wept, "I didn't mean to cry." I reached down in my purse to get out a tissue, and when I looked up, she was standing at the door.

"I have to go. Rehearsal is about to start."

That was the last thing she said to me for many years. She did not return my call the next day or my letter the following week. My other friend had a very different response.

When we spoke, she embraced me, apologized, and invited me over shortly thereafter.

One friendship was strengthened by the truth of my pain. The other was ended. But about situations like this, I like to remind myself: I didn't lose a friend, for friends would never be separated by tearful honesty. Today, I don't judge her for running away, but neither would I pursue her friendship. I cannot be a friend to anyone else until I befriend myself.

▶ PRIVATE RISKS

Finally, there are those private risks taken in the solitude of our rooms when we come face-to-face with the mirror of who we really are. Whether it's taking the time to pray, to cry, to remember, to set goals, to meditate, to journal, or to admit to a mistake, these can be life's greatest risks.

My greatest private risks have been confronting my binge eating, my charge card debting, and choosing separation and divorce.

Never be afraid of the dark.
It is only then that we can see the stars,
And in the beauty of the stars
We find our way.

Because of the work I do, hardly a week goes by that I don't meet someone who has demonstrated tremendous courage in the facing of his or her private demons. Years ago, I met a couple who shared an amazing story. Both were divorced when they met. Previously, he had admitted to a sexual addiction and sought counseling for it. After they were married, she chose to face her workaholism, leave her 65-hour-a-week management position, and go home to raise her one-year-old. As I listened, I heard great joy and pride in the fact that they were preparing to celebrate their tenth wedding anniversary.

The thief who faces his or her dishonesty, the alcoholic who stops drinking, the depressed parent who seeks counseling, a young woman who admits to an eating disorder, the employee who leaves a good job to start his own business: each is an example of how we can take private risks back to integrity and wholeness. These are life's unsung heroes.

A   *Be not afraid*

In a survey of 80–90 year olds, the group was asked which they regretted more, risks they had taken or risks they had not taken. Which would you guess was the almost unanimous response, the former or the latter?

Their greatest regrets were the risks they had not taken. The good news is, there is no need for regrets. You have not lost anything. There is only Now, and your Now is here, inviting you to live it fully.

▶ AM I FULLY ALIVE?

Risks don't always turn out as we had hoped, but they always bring greater insight and the reward of living every day to the fullest. When my oldest daughter was in the third grade, she came home one day from science class with an exciting insight. "Mom, do you know how you can tell if a plant is alive?"

"How?" I asked.

"If it's growing!"

I told her that is the same way you can tell if a person is alive. To be fully alive, we must take risks.

▶ LIFE WITHOUT RISK

When I was still in my 20's, my single aunt was twice my age, but we would often socialize together. One day, when I called to invite her to an outing, she informed me she was through with such things. "Don't ask me to any more singles' activities," she said. "I'm done with all that. I give up! I just want to stay home and be by myself.."

Less than a year later, on her fiftieth birthday, I was at her hospital bedside when the doctor told her she was full of inoperable cancer.

When the hospital chaplain walked into her room, his first question to her was, "Are you recently divorced or widowed?"

"I've never been married," she said through her tears.

"And how do you feel about that?"

"I've been bitter about it most of my life," she admitted.

"Let's start there," he said. I left the room amazed at how quickly he uncovered one of her core issues.

Isolation is the darkroom
where I develop my negatives.

Could my aunt's 'giving up' have increased her susceptibility to a disease such as cancer? Dr. Bernie Siegel reminds us that we must continue our personal growth, or we may find ourselves one day with a physical 'growth'. Part of this journey to wholeness is the huge risk of connecting with others.

(1)

Fear of Getting It

▶ THE BEGINNING RISK TAKER

It was shortly after one of my seminars on Freedom that a middle-aged gentleman who was a top manager at a Fortune 500 company came forward to ask me a question.

"Mary Kay, if a person wanted to begin taking risks again, where would he begin?"

His question caught me off guard. I started to mumble the titles of some books, but then decided instead to create for him the following list:

▷ **101 RISKS FOR THE BEGINNING RISK TAKER!** ◁

- Play Monopoly or checkers
- Go bike riding
- Play hopscotch
- Build a model
- Go for a walk
- Play tennis
- Volunteer someplace
- Swing on a swing
- Play the piano/harmonica
- Call a friend
- Lay on the ground and do cloud watching or snow angels
- Do leggos
- Play in the sprinkler
- Clean/paint/wallpaper your room
- Do a litter-pick-up somewhere
- Play with your pet
- Play cards
- Dance to music
- Write with chalk on the sidewalk
- Have a picnic
- Go swimming/sledding
- Make a fire and roast marshmallows
- Organize a drawer/closet
- Memorize a poem/the state capitals
- Go fishing
- Have a lemonade stand/car wash
- Have a garage sale
- Read a book
- Get a massage
- Plant a garden
- Invest in the stock market
- Sing in the shower
- Ask a new friend to dinner
- Go canoeing or sailing
- Do a summersault or cartwheel
- Ask for a raise
- Jetski or tube
- Cry or laugh
- Turn off the TV for a week
- Give someone a hug
- Hum on the escalator or shuttle bus
- Tell a joke
- Order something off the Internet
- Finger paint with a child or a friend
- Have your fortune told or your horoscope done
- Buy a bold tie/have your nails done/braid your hair
- Speak up with a question or comment in a group
- Journal your feelings for five minutes
- Go to a church service at a synagogue, mosque or church other than your own
- Rent a convertible or drive a stick shift
- Hold a baby or visit an infirm elderly person
- Write a letter to the editor/to a friend
- Make a list of 10 dreams and read it to someone
- Hang out for a day with someone not your age
- Go to a movie you don't think you'll like
- Get your picture taken in a photo booth
- Go to a batting cage or go-cart park
- Join Toastmasters or propose a toast at your next evening out
- Disagree with someone you usually agree with
- Go for the weekend to a large city

- Record a night-dream and tell someone about it
- Weigh yourself and tell someone
- Folk or square dance
- Ice skate/roller skate/roller blade
- Have a party
- Learn a magic trick
- Sit on the floor
- Whistle in public
- Pick out a beautiful stranger and go up and start a conversation
- Learn to cook something exquisite
- Stop someone at your work or place of worship and thank them
- Ask someone for their autograph
- Balance your checkbook to the penny
- Take a meditation or yoga or Tai Chi class
- Take a fencing or self-defense class
- Ride in an airplane or helicopter
- Jump or dive off a diving board
- Go snorkeling or scuba diving
- Try out for a play or play charades
- Sing in a choir or sing karaoke
- Tell someone your age
- While at work, close your eyes and breathe deeply for 30 seconds
- Go camping with a tent or under the stars
- Ask someone to do you a favor
- Write a letter to one of your heroes who is still living and mail it
- Set a limit or say "no"
- Pet a snake or hold a mouse
- Ride a horse or mule or donkey or elephant or camel
- Visit someone in the hospital or hospice
- Hit the airline attendant button on the plane and ask for something
- Ask a waitress/waiter for a specific food item or condiment
- Get a new hairdo or dye your hair or grow a moustache or beard
- Ride a roller coaster or Ferris wheel
- Tell a truth you've been hiding

- Have your aura picture taken
- Buy bubble gum and blow a bubble or blow soap bubbles
- Send someone flowers
- Write yourself a love letter
- Compliment someone at work on something specific
- Take a class or drop a class
- Play laser tag or freeze tag
- Talk to someone on the elevator
- Dress up for Halloween
- Donate blood
- Initiate a conversation at the grocery store or bus or airport
- Climb to the top of a tower or ride up a glass elevator
- Throw a frisbee
- Get on a chat room on the Internet
- Walk in the rain with your face up and no umbrella
- Paint, sculpt or water color
- Go to a store that is too expensive for you to buy anything
- Line Dance or Country Dance
- Change your answering machine message dramatically
- Walk through a zoo, forest or conservatory
- Put change in someone else's meter
- Ask someone for the time (on their watch) or directions
- Eat at a new ethnic restaurant
- Meet a new neighbor
- Jump rope or Hula Hoop
- Ride a motorcycle or an electric bike or scooter
- Share thanks aloud before a meal
- Step into a fountain
- Feed the pigeons, sea gulls, etc.
- Call into a radio show
- Write a magazine article
- Go sleeveless or wear shorts
- Tell someone you love them

Fear of Getting It

For each of us, different items from the risk list would be more or less challenging. The list is only meant to get you started, to help you feel more comfortable in your discomfort zone.

1. Which five new risks would be the easiest to take?

_____

_____

_____

_____

_____

2. Which five new risks would be the most difficult to take?

_____

_____

_____

_____

_____

3. Which of my answers from #2 would I be most willing to take? What would be my first step?

_____

_____

_____

_____

_____

In America, people pay thousands of dollars to take an outdoors course and have an hour to build an igloo on the mountaintop before their hands start to numb. We'll pay hundreds of dollars to jump off a bridge with a bungee cord strapped to our backs. We willingly spend a few more dollars to get on the wildest and fastest roller coaster in the theme park. Exciting risks. But those who get the most out of such experiences are the ones who use them as catalysts to take the real day-to-day risks of being fully alive in the present moment.

▶ FORMULA FOR MAKING DECISIONS

As I talk to people wanting a new level of happiness, I've found fear to be the most formidable enemy. My formula for making every decision is a simple one, *"If I had no fear, what would I do?"* I have never regretted the outcome! As we decide each day how much to risk, the most immediate question is not, "Is there life after death?" but "Is there life <u>before</u> death?"

Security is mostly a superstition.
Avoiding danger is no safer in the long run than outright exposure.
Life is either a daring adventure or nothing.

Helen Keller

Note that sometimes what we call risks, e.g., a teen getting drunk, a spouse having an affair, an employee up and quitting, are just cover-ups for not taking the real risks of honest, open communication. If your motivation for taking a risk is anger or frustration rather than joy and exhilaration, the 'risk' is most likely an avoidance tactic.

Answer each of these questions with 4–6 endings:

If I had no fear...

_____

_____

_____

_____

_____

_____

If I were convinced that I'm never given a dream without the power to make it come true...

_____

_____

_____

_____

_____

_____

Fear of Getting It

1

If I were to express the music inside of me...

_____

_____

_____

_____

_____

_____

_____

_____

_____

_____

Work like you don't need money.
Love like you've never been hurt.
Dance like no one's watching.

The Four Reasons We Run From Happiness:

☐ 1. Fear of Getting It

☑ **2. Fear of Losing It**

☐ 3. The Belief That We Don't Deserve It

☐ 4. Guilt

"If I got it, I'm afraid I might lose it!" is another popular excuse for not pursuing greater happiness. We can lose many things. The stock market could crash. Our home could be leveled by a tornado. The person we love might leave us. However, our level of happiness is not determined by having things or relationships. We cannot have happiness taken from us; we can only choose, consciously or unconsciously, to give it away.

> *It is not easy to find happiness in ourselves,*
> *and it is not possible to find it elsewhere.*
>
> Agnes Repplier

When we choose to let our fear of tomorrow's loss destroy our serenity today, what are we saying? "Since I might have a painful time a month from next Thursday, I'll just start being depressed today. Then when it comes, there's no big surprise." How much sense does that make?

▶ A STORY OF SELF-SABOTAGE

"I think I'm destroying something good because the pain of losing it would be more than I could bear." This amazing statement was uttered to me one evening by a beautiful 22-year-old. I asked her to explain.

She recounted that every Friday night for the past month her new boyfriend had driven an hour from his home to take her out. The week after she started my class, they were on their way to a restaurant when they had the following conversation:

"Boy, you sure smell good," she commented.

"Thanks," he said.

"I thought you came here right from work."

"I did."

"You wear cologne to work?" she asked.

He nodded. "A little. I put on extra for you."

"I've never known a guy to wear cologne to work. Do you have somebody on the side?"

At this point, he turned to her and said, "No, I've got three on the side. I've been meaning to tell you."

"You're playing with my mind," she retorted.

"No," he replied. "You are. Can you figure out why?"

She went on to explain that he was the most wonderful man she'd ever dated and how terrified she was of losing him. Once she recognized her underlying fear of loss and how it was affecting her, she had new homework, not to love him less, but to love herself more.

I have often found myself in relationships where I felt that if I did something very right or something very wrong, it would affect the outcome of the relationship. Rather than just being myself and trusting in my Higher Power to take care of the rest, I felt I had to control the outcome by changing my behaviors, my weight, or my children.

When we let our fears overtake us, our attempts to manage things and people appears as nagging, peevishness or insecure meddling. In short, rather than being attractive, we are reactive.

So, how do we handle fear? We focus on the positive and turn it over. Focusing on the positive means that we think about the things we are grateful for and how we are able to attract wonderful things into our lives. Turning it over means that we acknowledge that both the situation and ourselves are in God's hands. Even the worst that can happen could be a blessing.

▶ FEAR OF ROCK BOTTOM

Rock Bottom is the mental state where many of us landed on the night of our first big heartbreak or the day we missed out on a big job opportunity. Rock Bottom is the dark night of the soul. Its darkness comes not from the circumstances, but from the lies we choose to believe.

There are two beliefs that make Rock-Bottom so painful:

1. We believe that nothing we can ever do will improve our present situation or relieve our hurt.

2. We believe that no one has ever felt this way before, and therefore, we choose not to talk to others about it. We convince ourselves, "They just wouldn't understand."

These are two of life's greatest lies. Therefore, it is crucial that we counter them with these truths:

1. The light at the end of tunnel is always there, but sometimes, because we're going around a curve, we just can't see it.

2. Our pain is not 'special'. Everything we are facing has been faced before. Facing Rock Bottom experiences is the boot camp of life. After a wound, the skin that grows back is always stronger.

My rock bottoms have included break-ups and divorces, almost closing my business when I discovered we were up to our ears in debt, being kicked out of a musical revue with no warning because I was too 'bossy', having a girlfriend stop talking to me one day (and never tell me why), and losing my father to cancer. Each time I needed to express my feelings to someone close, and each one of them always reassured me that, eventually, everything would be all right. And so it was.

Look back on 4 or 5 of your rock bottoms.

How did you handle them? How did they turn out? Are you still holding onto the pain from any of them right now? Do you still believe that "No one would understand?"

_____

_____

_____

_____

_____

_____

_____

_____

_____

_____

_____

_____

_____

▶ THE LESSON AT THE BOTTOM

A few years ago, a man in his 40's came into my office and said, "I want to be just like you!" I assumed he didn't mean he wanted small ear lobes and fat knees, so I asked him what he meant.

"I want to be a high self-esteem person!" he exclaimed.

"Sorry," I said, "Everyone has low self-esteem days from time to time. But I can help you have more high self-esteem days. I call them 'A-Days.'"

A-days occur when we feel on top of the world; we're at our best and inviting the best from those around us. But occasionally we have B-Days

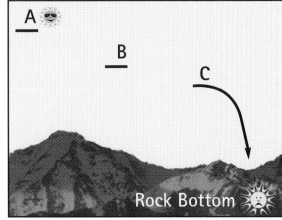

where little things go wrong, like a bad-hair day or a non-matching socks day. We can also have C-Days. The car dies. The fish dies. The relationship dies. Our hope dies.

When I am confronted by someone who is miserable, having weeks or months of C-Days, I remind him or her that taking risks is only way to get from a C-Day to a B or an A-Day. The gentleman in my office, realizing he was living a C-Day life, looked perturbed. "No way!" he said. "Taking risks is how I ended up this low!" I could see him building his little condo at C-level.

"But you're miserable!" I protested.

"You got that right," he said. "But this is my comfort zone." It was his *uncomfortable* comfort zone. I reminded him that he really had nothing to lose by taking a risk. The most miserable place for us is really at level C. (Remember the frogs in the pot of water?)

The fear of taking one more risk may be considerable, but if we succeed, we're up to level B. If we fail, we will hit the rocks and our pain will be so great, it will overshadow our fear of taking risks and we'll change. Once we take the action needed, we'll find ourselves at level A again.

When I was in the shelter, I didn't sit and ask, "Should I take a risk and change my life? I just can't decide." On the contrary, the decision was one of the easiest I've ever made. The pain I'd been experiencing was too intense for me to do otherwise.

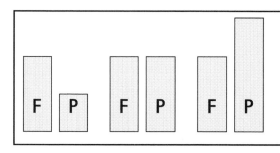

- *When we have More Fear than Pain, we stay in the situation.*
- *When we have Equal Fear and Pain, we talk about changing but don't do it.*
- *When we have More Pain than Fear, we shift.*

So what am I saying here? Do you need to wait until your next crisis to make a change? Hardly. If you do the exercises in this book and take a look at what's happening in your life and what you desire for yourself, the desire to change will surface naturally.

> *There came a day when the pain of staying in one place*
> *was greater than the pain of moving forward.*
>
> Anaïs Nin

1. Think back to the 5 happiest people you listed on page 22.

What do they have in common?

_____

_____

_____

_____

_____

_____

2. Have any of them themselves overcome a hardship such as loss of a loved one, loss of a business or home, overcoming an addiction or having a near-death experience?

_____

_____

_____

_____

_____

_____

3. Do most of them have lots of money, power, or fame?

_____

_____

_____

_____

_____

The longest laugh ever recorded for a live studio audience was for an episode of the Jack Benny show. Jack, known for being frugal with his funds, was in his home one evening when a burglar intruded. The burglar shouted, "Your money or your life." There was no reply for over a minute. When the burglar repeated the phrase, Benny simply said, "I'm thinking!"

Are you still thinking which is more important to you? If you tie up your happiness in money, fame, real estate or relationships, you may lose it. No study ever done has shown that increased wealth or fame increases long-term happiness. Nor has there been one to show that increased wealth means decreased worry about money matters.

The reason you aren't happy has never been, and will never be about money, fame or power. When we realize that we could lose everything in these categories tomorrow and still be happy, we will be able to freely accept happiness.

At various times in my life, my fear of losing happiness resulted in a sense of insecurity that often brought about the negative event I most wanted to avoid. Whether it concerned a relationship or the audition for an acting role, I was often my own greatest saboteur.

When I booked my first national speaking engagement, I recognized this fear and was able to face it head on.

Author John Rosemond had just invited me to be one of three speakers for his Center for Affirmative Parenting. His letter read, "I love your stuff! Let's go change the world together!" I was ecstatic, on a hope-filled 'high'.

Shortly thereafter, Rosemond called to inform me that my first audience would be "one of the toughest" – a Young President's Organization chapter. (YPO's are presidents of multi-million dollar businesses by the time they are forty.) I was to speak to this YPO assembly on a cruise ship off the coast of California. In the four hours I would be presenting to them, I would make or break my young career as a national speaker.

After Rosemond's call, I neither ate nor slept as I wrestled with my fear of losing his respect and embarrassing myself in front of the YPO's. Then I remembered a story I share with my audiences.

► The Story of the Two Millionaires

In a small Midwest town there lived two next-door neighbors, Harry and Ernie, who each headed successful million-dollar businesses. Harry had inherited his flourishing business from his father. Ernie had earned his from scratch.

Well, just when everything seemed to be humming along for both of them, along came a stock market crash. Instantly, both men lost their fortunes. Their friends and neighbors were very worried. To have lost so much! How would the two handle it? Finally, a small group of friends got together to visit the neighbors and see how each was faring.

What they discovered was that one of the former millionaires was – as they had feared – devastated. The other, however, was just fine and determined as ever to rebuild.

Who was devastated? Harry who had inherited the fortune, or Ernie, who had earned it? Your answer:

_____

Almost everyone agrees that the devastated man was Harry. He felt he was a 'victim' of luck – both good and bad – and was therefore disheartened by his loss. Ernie, on the other hand, knew he was the attractor of his good fortune. He knew what is known by all the world's happiest individuals: My greatest asset for achieving happiness is myself, with all my God-given talents and abilities. No one and no circumstance can take away this most precious resource.

So, how did my talk aboard the cruise ship go? Superbly. Once I realized I could walk off the ship with everything I had when I walked onto it (plus an additional good tan), I released the majority of my fear and anxiety.

No one can make you feel inferior without your consent.
                                            Eleanor Roosevelt

Many of us stay stuck in confusion and suffering because we fear the pain of loss. We forget that pain is our friend.

▶ THE GIFT OF PAIN

I recall a woman in her 50's who described herself as 'miserable'. Her source of pain, in her words, was that her husband didn't love her. I asked her if she knew that for a fact, or was only surmising it to be true. "Oh, I could never ask him," she replied. "I'd be too afraid of the answer."

Had this woman summoned the courage to ask, she might have been pleasantly surprised. Even if her husband had said, "No, I don't love you," her pain would have set her free. How? Either by allowing her to let go of wondering about his affection, or by igniting her anger and energizing her to take positive action such as falling in love with herself.

▶ BLESSING OR CURSE?

Did you know there is a physical disease in which those afflicted feel no pain? If it sounds like that wouldn't be so bad, think again. The disease is leprosy.

I learned about leprosy on a television series that aired during the '80's entitled *Magnum P.I.* It related the weekly adventures of a (really cute) single-guy private detective on a Hawaiian island.

In one episode, as Magnum's new girlfriend was walking along the beach barefooted with him, she shared that she had leprosy. Slowly the camera panned down to their feet as they approached a sharp, rusty, metal object protruding from the sand. Viewers watched as she unknowingly impaled her foot on the object, oblivious to the pain or the danger she faced.

Playfully, she then challenged Magnum to a race to the water. Splashing around in the ocean washed away any evidence of the injury. After a commercial, the program resumed with a somber scene. Magnum and a physician stood by the young woman's hospital bedside. "I'm afraid we didn't catch the infection in time to save the foot," the doctor said. "We'll have to amputate."

Lack of pain was the cause of the young woman's misfortune. Pain, whether physical or emotional, is every person's friend. But you wouldn't guess it from listening to ads in the media. "Get rid of your pain with PAIN-NO MORE," the messages promise. This is a dangerous mindset.

▶ PAIN IS OUR FIRE ALARM

Imagine reacting to a fire alarm, for example, by simply turning it off while the fire rages on. Yet when we take a pain-killer, we usually turn off that warning without investigating the source of the problem.

Fear of Losing It 2

Physical Pain: What are some aches, pains, itches or upsets that your body has been using lately to get your attention?

_____

_____

_____

_____

_____

_____

Take a moment to thank your body for these indications of stress. Go now to some part of your body where there has been an affliction. Send deep, loving breath to that area of your body. Be with it. Focus on it. Think of it as a hurting child trying to get your attention. Massage it with your hands or your loving, peaceful thoughts. Take some more deep breaths. Thank that part of your body for what it does for you. See it as perfect and whole, a part of a perfectly functioning mechanism.

What are you noticing?

_____

_____

_____

_____

_____

_____

Emotional Pain: What are some painful emotions that have been present in you recently?

_____

_____

_____

_____

_____

Take a moment to thank your being for these signals. Release judgment. Be with the feelings for a few minutes, allowing yourself to feel them. Notice that they, like the physical pain, move through you, sometimes in waves. Surround them with the light of your awareness. Breathe.

What are you noticing?

_____

_____

_____

_____

_____

_____

▶ JUST SAY 'YES'

We tell our youth, "Just say 'No' to drugs." A much more powerful and appropriate message would be, "Just say 'Yes' to feeling and respecting your pain." Words are not enough, however. Young people need to not only hear this message, but they need to see us honoring our pain for the important news it bears that there is something, somewhere, in our lives that is not in alignment with the truth.

Over the years I have heard dozens of stories about the extraordinary lengths we go to in order to avoid pain. One in particular that stands out occurred in a small non-profit corporation. The secretary of this company had, over the course of a year, embezzled over $12,000 from the business to 'help out' her boyfriend.

Although there were many warning signs that this activity was occurring, the small staff chose to avoid the pain of confrontation, in hopes the problem was not real or would somehow take care of itself. The staff rescued her as she had rescued her boyfriend, until the problem reached crisis stage. At that point her behaviors came to light, she was fired, and the company was forced to move to a smaller office in order to survive.

This scenario is a common one. Not only do we get ourselves into messes because we are afraid of the painful changes in our lives, but we often go to great lengths to rescue others from the pain of reality and growth as well.

▶ THE RESULTS OF RESCUING

I once saw an excellent example of the ill effects of rescuing on the popular television talk show, *Oprah*.

The world-renowned host was interviewing some mothers who had repeatedly loaned money to their adult children despite the lack of payments in return. Both the mothers and the children were sitting on stage. One mother had a son in college who had borrowed large amounts of money for such items as a boat, a truck, ski-equipment, and jewelry for his girlfriend.

Another mother had repeatedly loaned money to her 25-year-old son and was now suing him to get it back. Oprah pointed out, "You don't all of a sudden get to be 25 and irresponsible. I'm sure, as his mother, you have seen the signs all through his adolescence that he was irresponsible. So why would you make a loan to somebody who is irresponsible?"

"If we hadn't loaned him the money the second time, he might have gone to jail," replied the mother.

"You should have let him go to jail," challenged an audience member. Instead of facing the immediate pain of a few days behind bars, the young man was suffering through the humiliation of hearing his mother reproach him in front of millions of television viewers.

Rescuing people from the natural consequences of their behaviors never helps them or us. When we rescue others from pain, the result is always worse than the pain we were attempting to help them avoid. Tough love of a child is difficult but necessary. In the past, many parents used the excuse, "We can't afford it," to keep balance in family life. Today this is often just not true. Parents must simply say, "No."

▶ TIME FOR TOUGH LOVE

A woman called me a few months ago to see if I knew of any good career counselors for her daughter who was out of work. "How old is your daughter?" I asked.

"Twenty-six."

"Then she's living at home with you and pays no room or board."

"Of course she can't pay us room and board, she has no job," said the mother.

"Since you called to ask for my assistance, here's the most helpful thing I can tell you: Charge her $25 per month for room and board starting the first of next month, then double it every month until she moves out. If she can't pay and won't move out, put her belongings in the driveway. If after 24 hours they're still there, call the Salvation Army to pick them up. Any questions?"

She couldn't think of any.

▶ KEEPING YOUR WORD

I have heard dozens of stories of complete turn-arounds when a parent set a clear limit. As parenting author John Rosemond once stated in a lecture, "It really doesn't matter much what your boundaries are. Set the curfew at 11, 12 or 1, the child will still break it. The question is, `Do you keep your word?'"

If we want our children to say NO to drugs, sex, gangs, etc., we must model for them how to set limits, no matter how challenging it may be to hold to them. We are reminded that in life, *pain is required, suffering is optional.*

▶ No Safety in Security

I once had a manager say to me, "I've created a security blanket that is suffocating me." When we choose to move toward joy rather than away from pain, the result is exhilaration and vitality. The concept of loss is an inaccurate assessment. The concept of security is an illusion. The more we concentrate on playing it safe, the less we have to celebrate.

Be like the bird that, passing on her flight awhile on boughs too slight,
feels them give way beneath her, and yet sings,
knowing that she hath wings.

Victor Hugo

The Belief that We Don't Deserve It

(3)

The Four Reasons We Run From Happiness:

☐ 1. Fear of Getting It

☐ 2. Fear of Losing It

☑ 3. The Belief that We Don't Deserve It

☐ 4. Guilt

> *A man cannot be comfortable without his own approval.*
> *The worst loneliness is not to be comfortable with yourself.*
>
> Mark Twain

The notion that somehow we are not deserving of a life of joy is the most common reason we avoid happiness and often the most difficult thinking pattern to transform. Therefore, as we begin to see through this fallacy, the truth has tremendous healing power.

Imagine you have been asked to address 500 high school students tomorrow on the topic of "How to Deserve Happiness."

What would your main points be?

_____

_____

_____

_____

_____

_____

_____

_____

_____

Would your message be a short one or a long one?

_____

To be happy, I used to believe that I had to be free from flaws; 99.44% pure, like the old Ivory Soap commercials. Since such perfection is unattainable, such beliefs condemn us to a life of misery. Would we require similar standards of our children before we allowed them the right to happiness?

Hardly.

There are only two possible answers to the question of who deserves happiness:

We all have a birthright to happiness by our very existence.

OR

No one deserves happiness. It is a free gift. We must simply open up our arms to embrace it.

It sounds so simple, yet still we resist. Most of us want to recite a litany of reasons why we are undeserving. For one person, the reason is a disastrous mistake made years ago. For another, it's something bad that's been done to him or her. For a third, it's a compilation of all the little mistakes made in life that together build a mountain of unworthiness. We can distort and magnify our brokenness to the point of paralysis.

> *Rebellion against your handicaps gets you nowhere.*
> *Self-pity gets you nowhere. One must have the adventurous daring to accept*
> *oneself as a bundle of possibilities and undertake the most interesting game in the*
> *world — making the most of one's best.*
>
> Harry Emerson Fosdick

▶ JANE'S STORY

A good friend of mine, I'll call her Jane, was very unhappy in her marriage. When Jane discovered her husband's repeated unfaithfulness, she decided to take her young son and move from California back home to Iowa.

Suddenly, the husband's mistresses didn't look so good to him.

Cards and letters, flowers and gifts began arriving at Jane's home daily. But none of these received a warm response, including the final telegram that read, "I cannot live without you." Three days later, she received a call saying her ex-husband had attempted suicide.

In Jane's mind, this was her ultimate proof that she did not deserve happiness. She had taken a vow to love and honor her mate "till death do us part," and now she felt responsible for almost ending his life.

Her owning responsibility for his actions had serious negative effects. A year later, Jane's smoking had increased and her weight decreased to a point where her family practically forced her into a retreat weekend for separated and divorced individuals. She reluctantly agreed to go.

When she arrived at the retreat site, Jane was horrified to discover that her small group leader was a minister. She recalls thinking, "Don't these people know God doesn't care for my kind?" She had reached her Rock Bottom.

During the first small group discussion, the clergyman asked the woman seated next to Jane to share something about herself with the group. The woman began, "Five years ago, my ex-husband attempted suicide, and I've never really been able to forgive myself since."

Jane started to reach out to reassure the woman that it was not her fault. As she did, she watched in amazement as everyone, including the minister, reached out as well. Witnessing this outpouring of love for someone in her own situation, Jane began to cry uncontrollably. Her tears broke the dam of self-reproach that had held her prisoner all those months.

With the help of her weekend retreat, Jane was able to forgive herself and gently close the door on her past. Today, she is happily remarried.

We all live with the objective of being happy;
our lives are all different and yet the same.

Anne Frank

▶ Who Is 'Self-Centered'?

Someone once asked me if my classes on self-empowerment puffed everyone up and made them think they were better than anyone else. I responded that I had met only one person who seemed to think he was better than everyone. It was a man who was adamant that everyone should know that he had the IQ of a genius. He was also a homeless alcoholic.

On the other hand, nearly every day I meet people who think they are *worse* than everyone else. It is this group of individuals that fits my definition of self-centeredness. These individuals give very little to others because they believe they have nothing to give. Their fixation with their own feelings of inadequacy, fear, and guilt consumes the time and energy they could be using to share their gifts with the world.

As long as we believe *our* brokenness is the greatest, we are caught in a web of suffering. A good phrase for all of us might be, "My pain is ordinary." Such a belief would help us to live extraordinary lives.

▶ Healing the Wounds

Bad things happen to everyone. If we do not let the wounds of these events heal, their memory may fester within us for years. In consequence, hanging on to a victim mindset often leads to disastrous results.

Suppose that three days ago you fell down and scraped your forearm badly. Today you find yourself chatting with a group of friends describing how awful the wound looked. As you talk, you realize that the wound has started to heal, but you want to make your point clear, so you reopen the scab, pulling it back to show your friends.

What would be the long-term effects of such action if repeated over time?

_____

_____

_____

_____

_____

_____

Describe people you have known who reopen their emotional wounds week after week or year after year.

What are the effects of their choices?

_____

_____

_____

_____

_____

_____

What wounds are you holding onto that are still a part of your self-definition?

Jot down how long you have been holding onto each.

_____

_____

_____

_____

_____

_____

Imagine forgiving yourself or these other people for all of the above, never sharing the stories again with anyone.

What comes up for you?

_____

_____

_____

_____

_____

_____

(More on forgiveness in the chapter on Habit B!)

We often fall into a victim thinking pattern without realizing it. We open old wounds to talk about them 'one more time'. But just as the body cannot heal if wounds are constantly reopened, emotional and spiritual healing are inhibited if our inner wounds are revisited. The 'infection' resulting from reopened wounds often causes a festering that is worse than the original problem.

> *A fool sees not the same tree that a wise man sees.*
> William Blake

We have all made mistakes and been the recipient of others' mistakes. Forgiveness is not forgetting. It is accepting that *we were all doing the best we could at the time with the information we had.* Forgiveness of yesterday is necessary to attain real freedom and joy today.

During my time at the shelter, I realized I had never forgiven myself for being imperfect. I had a mental list of all the things I wanted to 'fix' about myself. Once I realized the list was never going to diminish in size, I had a new decision to make:

I could continue to berate myself and hold back self-acceptance until I was 'fixed', creating more misery and self-deprecation for the rest of my life,

OR

I could accept that I was a broken vessel, and learn to love and honor myself despite my cracks and chips.

I chose the latter. Shortly thereafter, I realized that the only way that I could stop trying to fix me was to envision myself as eternally 'unfixable'. That is why I created a new paradigm and resolved to start seeing myself as: Half-Jerk/Half-Jewel.

► HALF-JERK/HALF-JEWEL

As I started to become comfortable with this concept, I realized there were two important rules associated with it:

The ratio would never change, no matter how hard I tried to change myself. It would always be 50/50.

At their core everyone was exactly the same as I was.

This paradigm shift altered me, freed me. I relaxed. I became more honest about my shortcomings, accepted compliments more graciously, and stopped looking down on myself, or up to other people. I forgave myself more quickly. I forgave them more quickly.

This helped me become more patient (I still have a long way to go!) and less prone to compare myself with others. No matter how handsome or beautiful, intelligent or powerful others look to me, I now know there is a 'jerk' lurking within everyone that needs healing and love just as I do. And no matter how cruel or callous another might appear to be, I now know there is a jewel waiting within to be discovered and cherished.

What you do not own, owns you.

Debbie Ford

Before you continue, take a moment to complete this phrase two or three times: "I'd be happier if only…"

_____

_____

_____

_____

_____

_____

_____

All answers to the above sentence completion fall into one of two categories.

Something impossible to change, such as, "…if I were taller," or "…if I had different parents."

OR

A habit or characteristic which can be changed, such as, "…if I lost some weight" or "…if I stopped procrastinating."

▶ 1: Accepting What I Cannot Change

This phrase from the first line of the *Serenity Prayer* reminds us that there are certain givens in life that we can perceive as blessings or barriers. Recently I was addressing a group of young single Moms and asked them to complete the "Life would be better" phrase. One-half of the group wrote down, "If only my baby's father were still around."

It was reality therapy time. "I could be happy if only" thinking is dangerous for the spirit who wants to live in the present. 12-step groups also have a phrase, "Living life on life's terms." Once our whining ceases, we can begin to see the possibilities in the moment at hand.

> *If you cannot find the truth right where you are,*
> *Where do you expect to find it?*
>
> Dogen

▶ 2: Changing What I Can

The four steps to changing our lives are simple, but not always easy. They are the 4 A's:

(A) **Awareness:** Seeing what is.

When we stop running and slow down to take a look at our lives, we see both gifts and challenges that we never knew were there.

(A) **Acceptance:** Owning what is.

Once we see our gifts and challenges, we can choose to accept responsibility for them, rather than projecting them onto others.

(A) **Accurate Assessment:** Clearing our I-sight

Once we have seen and accepted what is, we are confronted with the lies in our heads that have kept us from taking action.

(A) **Action:** Adjusting our thinking and the resulting behaviors

When we move beyond the old inaccurate assessments programming, we have a clear path to our new creation.

In working with clients, I find that the first two steps are the biggest ones. Once we can see a problem, such as weight, debt, overwork, etc., and own them as self-created, it is a short hop into a life change. The only stumbling block then is that in order to avoid the happiness we have longed for, our mind conjures up all sort of lies about how if we once solve the problem, things will get worse! To illustrate, let me share with you John's story as an example of how to use these four steps:.

John was a man in his 30's, living in a shelter where I was speaking one December. John began the class complaining about being extremely chilled at night with only one blanket on his bed. Despite not sleeping well because he was so cold, he was unwilling to ask for an additional blanket. His 4 A's looked like this:

(A) **Awareness** = "I am cold with only one blanket."

The group helped John narrow the scope of the problem to a manageable size. It wasn't 'the world' or 'this place' that was the problem. It was the lack of an additional blanket causing lack of sleep. He also became aware that, as a result, his work was suffering. His sleepiness impaired his concentration, and he was in danger of losing the job he needed to become independent again.

Acceptance = "I have the power to change the situation."

John admitted that complaining about everyone else wasn't helping. Therefore, he somewhat hesitantly owned that the person who needed to do some changing was himself.

(A) **Accurate Assessment** = "I can correct my errors in thinking."

Catching his pessimistic beliefs and turning them around was key. His belief was, "They kick you out for askin' for stuff like that!" When I asked where he got his information, he said someone at the last shelter he was in made it clear that such requests were taboo. Our class disputed John's thinking with evidence that this shelter's staff did not evict people for asking for what they needed in a courteous manner.

(A) **Action** = "I will ask for what I want."

Using the skills discussed in the chapter on Habit A in this book, John asked to speak to the night clerk, who responded, "How many blankets do you want?" John's entire thinking pattern was changed by the event, and he was able to graduate from the shelter program and finish his college education within two years.

A single event can awaken within us a stranger totally unknown to us.

Antoine de Saint-Exupery

Oftentimes, when we are blaming about some external problem outside of ourselves, it is really an internal change that needs to occur. Years ago I came across Nathaniel Branden's sentence completion exercise which is a tremendous help in getting to the core issue quickly. The process is simple — when you have a challenge that you believe is 'beyond your control', you simply complete the phrase: "The good thing about..."

Branden suggests you complete it 6–10 times. Often, it's on my very first completion that I get a powerful new Awareness. When I'm coaching individuals who are facing issues such as too busy, too poor, too overweight, etc., I see their breakthroughs as well. Some of their journaling or spoken answers have illuminated amazingly InAccurate Assessments!

The good thing about:

      No free time? ⟹   I don't have to deal with my problems
                           OR feelings
                           OR memories.

The Belief that We Don't Deserve It

3

Not enough money? ➡ At least I won't become greedy
OR all rich people are immoral
OR I'd probably go back to drinking.

Not losing weight? ➡ I won't have to handle all the attention
OR I'd be promiscuous
OR if I had heart attack, at least I wouldn't
have to grow old.

Procrastinating? ➡ It's a rush; I love the energy I get from deadlines
OR I don't have to do it 'perfectly' if I wait till
the last minute.

Complete the following:

The good thing about the situation I seem to be stuck in right
now is... (6–10 endings)

_____

_____

_____

_____

_____

_____

_____

_____

_____

My InAccurate Assessments seem to be that (e.g., all thin people
are immoral)

_____

_____

_____

_____

_____

What is one thing I've been complaining about that I could take Action on this week?

_____

_____

▶ CAN IT BE CHANGED?

To understand the harder-to-change category of 'if onlys', it is necessary to refer back to the Half-Jerk/Half-Jewel concept. When I ask teenage girls to complete the "I'd be happier of only..." phrase, they most often respond with, "If only I were prettier!"

"I believe every gift in our life has an inherent shortcoming," I challenge them. "What might be a challenge of being stunningly beautiful? The more beauty I have, the less I'd probably have of what other gift?"

It sometimes takes the girls a minute, but usually their consensus is 'personality'. I tend to agree. Beautiful women have an obvious and wonderful gift, but they usually aren't the best at making new friends. They have not needed to develop this skill, because as soon as they walk into a room, people are drawn to them.

How about the ability to tell a joke? Do we expect to see a Miss America contest where five of the ten finalists do stand-up comedy routines? It is highly unlikely, as they've never had to learn to hold someone's interest by being funny. They hold it by their loveliness.

What are some things about yourself that you could change if you really wanted to?

_____

_____

_____

_____

_____

_____

_____

Can you accept that you really don't want to change them, and release self-judgment?

_____

3 The Belief that We Don't Deserve It

What is there in your life that you cannot change but would like to?

_____

_____

_____

_____

_____

_____

_____

What are some of the possible gifts in this challenge? (If you get stuck, ask family and friends)

_____

_____

_____

_____

_____

_____

_____

Another good example of the Half-Jerk/Half-Jewel concept is the tendency towards right-brain or left-brain dominance. The more right-brained we are, the more creative and spontaneous we tend to be. The more we function out of our left brain, the more organized and analytical we will probably be. It is a continuum:

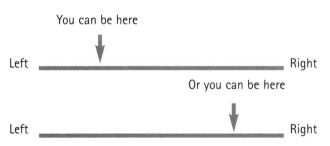

...or you can be anywhere on the continuum, but you cannot be in two places. Every time we move closer to one end, we lose out in the other category. As a strong right-brained person, (90% right, 10% left) I tend to be messier, and nonchalant about being ten minutes late for a lunch date. Yet on a good day, I can write a talk, an article and a song.

Do I want to trade places with my more left-brained (30% right, 70% left) office assistant? No! Does she want to trade places with me? Never! Nor would either of us want to give up some of our gift area in order to be precisely in the middle. I have, however, met individuals who are in the middle and just as content with being where they are, grateful for their unique gift of balance.

We each have different gifts and different weaknesses, but they all add up to an equally whole person. The goal is to be always grateful for the person that we are. (Note: 'Whole' is where the word 'Holy' comes from.)

Would you be rather whole or good?
Carl Jung

▶ THAT SMARTS!

What about extremely intelligent individuals? Early in my speaking career, I met Steve, a freshman in high school. He came up to me after one of my talks to ask a question. "I'm the smartest one in my class," he said, sincerely concerned. "What is my weakness?"

While Steve and I went for a walk, I told him I appreciated his openness. "Let's look at the gifts of people whom the world calls 'slow'," I suggested.

We came up with examples, such as a Down's syndrome child. We could see that such children often have big loving hearts, are nonjudgmental, laugh more easily, and have more patience. "Do you lack any of these gifts?" I asked him.

"I'm very impatient, and sometimes quite critical. That's it!" he concluded. Then he thanked me and left. If only we were all so willing to face our shortcomings.

Knowing others is wisdom, knowing yourself is Enlightenment.
Lao-tzu

Pick one or two of your "weaker areas." What is their gift side? (If you have trouble with this, ask your friends or family to help you.)

_____

_____

_____

_____

_____

The Belief that We Don't Deserve It

3

▶ NOT WANTING TO BE NOSEY

Most of my life, the thorn in my side was the nose on my face. I hated it from the first time I saw it in a three-way mirror when I was twelve. I truly thought God had made a mistake. So you can imagine how I felt twenty years later when I was offered a chance to fix the 'unfixable'. I was having dinner with my sister and her new boyfriend, who happened to be one of the top plastic surgeons in the country. Just as we began our dessert, he paused and leaned over to say, "I could do great things with that nose of yours." He was even going to give me a discount!

I seriously considered the offer for a few seconds before responding with, "I'm kind of attached to it, but thanks!"

At the time, I wasn't sure why I turned down such an opportunity, but about a year later that reason revealed itself. A gentleman walked up to me after a service at our church and said, "Your solo was beautiful today, Mary Kay. You must get down on your knees every night and thank God for that nose!"

I looked at him in shock. "What are you talking about?"

"You understand the resonance the shape of your nose gives, don't you? Didn't it ever occur to you why Barbra Streisand didn't get a nose job?"

It never had.

My voice is one of the gifts I am most grateful for. I truly cannot imagine life if I couldn't sing to comfort myself, to praise God, or to wake my kids up in the morning. And to think I almost ruined my gift because it was attached to a 'weakness'.

▶ SPECIALLY GIFTED

At the Seattle Special Olympics a few years ago, nine young contestants lined up for the 100-yard dash. Adrenaline coursing through their bodies, the runners took their starting positions. At the gun, all took off, except one boy whose cleats got caught in the starting block, causing him to fall. When he cried out in pain, all eight of the other runners ran back to help him. Then together, arm in arm, they crossed the finish line. The cheering for all those winners continued for over 10 minutes.

Imagine the uproar if one of our runners at the regular Olympics would stop to help up a competitor! Competitive and cooperative are *both* gifts!

I now see that no matter what characteristics we manifest, there are equal benefits to each:

My daughter isn't competitive	⟷	she's cooperative
My son isn't patient	⟷	he's enthusiastic
My friend isn't spontaneous	⟷	she's organized
I'm not the best at details	⟷	I'm a visionary

Each gift is important and beautiful in its own way. We complete each other.

▶ Educating Our Children

What do we teach our children? We teach them that two and two make four and that Paris is the capital of France. When will we also teach them who they are? We should say to each of them: "Do you know what you are? You are a marvel. You are unique. In all the years that have passed, there has never been another child like you. Your legs, your arms, your clever fingers, the way you move. You may become a Shakespeare, a Michelangelo, a Beethoven. You have the capacity for anything. Yes, you are a marvel. And when you grow up, can you then harm another who is, like you, a marvel?"

You must work; we all must work — to make the world worthy of its children.

Pablo Casals

▶ THE VIRTUE OF HUMILITY

How does the Half-Jerk/Half-Jewel theory fit in with the virtue of humility? It is my contention that this is the only formula that permits healthy humility.

If you believe you are less than Half-Jerk/Half-Jewel, you are judging yourself too harshly and comparing yourself negatively to those around you. Once you have done this to yourself, it is a short step to judging others. True humility is not the belief that you are worse than someone, but that you are no better than anyone. The only way to come to the latter conclusion is to accept that we are all equal in both gifts and brokenness.

I have never seen a greater monster or miracle in the world than myself.

Montaigne

So why don't we all act out our brokenness to the same degree? Because some of us accept it. Surprisingly, the key to abating the negative within us is not to like it, but to own it. Nathaniel Branden once wrote, "What we resist persists."

By the same token, the negatives we accept diminish.

Think of someone you admire. Choose someone who is (or was) in your life, rather than someone you have merely read about. Write down two or three of their admirable qualities.

_____

_____

_____

_____

Next, think of someone who drives you up a wall or gets under your skin.

Write down two or three of the most irritating qualities in this individual.

_____

_____

_____

_____

▶ JUDGE NOT

If the Half-Jerk/Half-Jewel formula is true, then why do we so readily put some people on pedestals and others in the dungeon? We do this by a process that psychologists call projection.

Mental health professionals identified projection just a few decades ago, but it is based on the age-old wisdom that what we admire and despise most in others is also found in ourselves to some degree. We project our denied faults and gifts onto the 'screen' of this other person, thereby enlarging what is there to the level of negative traits or positive traits. The cure is awareness.

> *The greatest of all faults is to be conscious of none.*
>
> Thomas Carlyle

For example, everyone is a tad bit irresponsible and dishonest. When we can accept that in ourselves, we become more responsible and more honest rather than projecting it onto 'enemies'. Mother Teresa was humble, yet she was the first to thank God for her gifts. She was humble because she owned her weaknesses. True humility is staying aware of our brokenness and refraining from judging the brokenness of others.

Every time we are deeply bothered by an action that we judge as wrong, we have imitated it. When we hang onto some anger concerning a bothersome characteristic in someone else, we are revealing our own lack of self-acceptance in this area.

Many Aboriginal tribes have a ritual at each full moon. Gathered around an evening campfire, they look across their circle to the person opposite them to become aware of whatever they admire most and judge most about the person. Then they look within to accept those positive and negative qualities in themselves. Thus, their attitudes are safe from projection.

> *Self-understanding rather than self-condemnation*
> *is the way to inner peace.*
>
> Joshua Loth Liebman

For the next 7 days, keep a running tally of the times you exhibited the qualities you wrote down in the last writing exercise. Keep breathing! And write your insights here:

_____

_____

_____

_____

_____

_____

_____

_____

_____

3

The Belief that We Don't Deserve It

For one woman who attended our seminar, the insight was sudden.

"What I despise in my brother-in-law is that he spends money like it's water!"

I asked her if it was her money he was spending.

"Of course not!"

"Then why does it bother you so much that he spends his own money?"

"It's irresponsible!" she exclaimed.

"Are *you* ever irresponsible?"

At that she gasped, covered her heart, took a step away from me and said, "I try not to be!"

What was she stepping back from and covering up? Every audience member I've asked since admits that they are at times irresponsible. When we resist Awareness and Acceptance, Action cannot flow.

> *At whatever point you judge another person,*
> *it is you who do the very same thing.*
>
> Romans 2:2

Different gifts are the spice of life. We need not envy others for what we do not have, for we have a gift which they do not. Each of our gifts carries with it a corresponding shortcoming, and each of our weaknesses holds a balancing strength. Once we realize this, self-comfortableness sets in and joy is close at hand.

The Belief that We Don't Deserve It

3

Imagine your best friend sending you a letter confessing every terrible thing he or she has ever been a victim of or done. The amazing coincidence is that this is exactly what has happened to you in your life. At the end of the letter, your friend begs forgiveness and asks if you are still willing to be friends. Write a reply to this friend now.

_____

_____

_____

_____

_____

_____

_____

_____

_____

_____

_____

_____

_____

_____

Will you deny your friend happiness or love as a result of his or her shortcomings?

_____

Do people have to be perfect to be happy?

_____

Do you need to wait for the whole world to be happy in order for you to be happy?

_____

3 The Belief that We Don't Deserve It

Do you need to wait for your people (community, sect, race, etc.) to be happy in order to be happy?

_____

Do you need to wait for your spouse and or children to be happy in order to be happy?

_____

The choice is yours.

_____

St. Iraneus once wrote, "Joy is the infallible sign of the presence of God." Neither God nor Joy have to be deserved, they simply need to be welcomed and embraced. Both are right here, in the present moment, awaiting our discovery and openness.

> *I do not have to earn love. I am loveable because I exist.*
> *Others reflect the love I have for myself.*
>
> Louise L. Hay

 ▶ IN REVIEW

To find happiness, we must release these two enemies: fear and judgment. We have discussed the first three reasons we run from happiness:

1. We fear getting it.

2. We fear losing it.

We have seen that these fears are inaccurate assessments.

3. We judge ourselves unworthy.

We have seen this judgment is inaccurate as well.

We must now look at our guilt and shame, which are the fourth and final reason we run from happiness. They include both fear (of scarcity) and judgment (of self).

4 Guilt

The Four Reasons We Run From Happiness:

☐ 1. Fear of Getting It

☐ 2. Fear of Losing It

☐ 3. The Belief that We Don't Deserve It

☑ 4. Guilt

Innocence: purity, virtue, spotlessness, blamelessness, honesty, simplicity, guiltlessness.

This final reason why we run from happiness makes as little logical sense as the first three, yet it is also extremely common. Just the other day, a young woman came up to me after a seminar and bemoaned, "If I were really happy, I wouldn't feel like my mother's daughter!" After we had a good laugh, she bought this book for her Mom!

> *My Mother is a Travel Agent for Guilt Trips.*
> Refrigerator magnet

Ever heard the phrase, 'If Momma ain't happy, ain't nobody happy'? It is a wonderful reminder that unhappiness and misery are often contagious. Why then, do we ever feel guilty about being happy?

▶ A God Who Loves Suffering

I find part of the answer in our interpretations of the teachings of certain religions. As a Catholic, for example, I was taught to give up whatever I liked best during Lent so I could grow in holiness. Although there are benefits to choosing abstinence, as a child I could not see the potential of inner focus but instead each Lent I looked for ways to increase my pain level. In fourth grade, my girlfriend and I jumped barefooted on the rocks behind school in near freezing temperatures in order to be 'holier'. I had come to the conclusion that God required suffering as a sign of our sincerity.

For others this belief lingers to this day. A few years back a man I'll call Ben went to see a priest because he had fallen in love with a young Catholic woman and wanted to know about her faith. In a 15-minute interview, one of the priest's axioms was, "And if you are too happy, you're not doing God's will." Fortunately, this is not a teaching of the Catholic Church, but one man's interpretation.

Recently, while working with another priest to prepare a Lenten television program, I heard him rephrase the concept of Lenten sacrifice beautifully for our audience. "This year, my friends, don't give up something that makes you happy. Give up something that makes you sad."

Guilt over happiness and 'If it feels good, it's bad' thinking are not limited to Catholics. Everywhere I go, I run into people who still believe such notions.

I remember the day a very excited gentleman wearing a three-piece suit walked into one of our seminars. "I'm so glad I finally get to take this class!" he said as I welcomed him.

"Great!" I said. "What kept you from attending before now?"

"I just wasn't ready. But today I registered at the university to begin my graduate classes. I'm going to get my master's degree in social work."

"What *have* you been doing?" I asked.

"Law. Hated it for years. But Mom always wanted an attorney, and I had the grades, and since I was the youngest of four sons... Well, once you get the degree, you feel like you gotta use it."

"So what was it that helped you finally follow your dreams after all these years?"

"Oh, Mom passed away about six months ago."

As parents we often unwittingly pressure our children to live out *our* dreams to "make something of themselves." The message we send to them is often, "I have paid the price of misery so you can be happy." Children do not follow our talk, they follow our walk. Our talk says, "I want you to be happy. " Our walk says, "Happiness is not a free gift. It is a bargain I have made for you. You must follow my definition of happiness in order to repay your debt to me." Nothing could be further from the truth or more harmful.

> *Guilt: The judgment or belief that there is something wrong*
> *about what you have done.*
> *A learned behavior. An unmet need for approval.*

> Iyanla Vanzant

▶ ARE YOU GUILTY?

With guilt as our guide, we can find numerous excuses to run from happiness. Here are three of the most common:

▶ 1. All or Nothing Thinking
"I care about people, so I will never be happy until they're happy." This common escape clause is a prescription for world-wide misery. The poor will always be among us, as will those addicted to drugs, gambling, food and complaining. Joining the ranks of the miserable in the name of guilt-ridden love is a most unloving decision, since we will simply spread what we most want to avoid!

Instead, we can use the unhappiness we see to contrast with what we are choosing for our own lives, and affirm those thoughts and feelings that return gratitude and joy back into our consciousness.

▶ 2. Loyalty to Those Without
"He sold out," is a remark I hear every once in a while from inner city teens. They are referring to those who have become financially successful. Such individuals are sometimes labeled and ostracized, as though their achievements are somehow disloyal to the community from which they came.

Another alternative was exemplified by a young woman who came up after a presentation I'd given. She shared, "I've been living in poverty for years. I'm a single parent, and that's what my family expected of me. Now I realize my affluence will in no way be harmful to them. In fact, I can be a model of where we all can go." (She became an instructor for me a few months later and started sharing her wonderful message.)

▶ 3. Belief in Scarcity

We often believe, "If I don't suffer, someone else will have to." This infers that there is only so much happiness to go around. It's called scarcity thinking. I used to believe there were only so many good men out there, so I got jealous every time a friend found one. In the meantime, if I won an award or was recognized, I often felt guilty because I was 'taking it away' from someone else just as deserving. As I became aware of my scarcity issues, my life changed for the better.

I now affirm that my happiness does not detract from the happiness of others. Likewise, their happiness can turn into a kind of Green-thumb-envy where I see myself experiencing whatever I desire in them, so that my 'ground' becomes fertile for its reception.

▶ WHEN OTHERS WANT TO GUILT US

Others' behaviors are only mirrors of how we treat ourselves. Therefore, as you release feeling guilty, others will cease suggesting that you are guilty. The following phrase is helpful, however, during that in-between time when perfect healing has not yet occurred. When someone is telling you in no uncertain terms that you have made the wrong choice, simply share with them in a calm and serene voice:

I acknowledge your desire to have me feel guilt around this issue.
I will let you know if I change my mind.

"But isn't guilt necessary to let us know when we're off the track?" you may ask.

As pointed out in Donald Neale Walsh's book, *Conversations with God, Book 3*, it's important to distinguish between awareness and guilt. Awareness opens our eyes and our intuition to a sense of when some act or circumstance does not feel good to us. We can learn to sense when that is the case and to act accordingly.

The other options are to hear what our inner wisdom says and do the opposite. (Our wisdom is patient. It can wait. You'll be back.) Or, because its advice is not acceptable in the circles in which you run, you can shut down your ability to listen to the inner wisdom that tells you what is in your best interest.

But for none of these options do we need to feel guilt. We will get what we give out. It's a fact of the universe. We don't need to feel guilty about asking for more of the same to be returned to us, any more than we need to feel proud of it. If we want to feel proud or guilty, we may do so. We simply return to the question, "What feels good to feel or to think or to believe?"

4

Guilt

1. Which gifts in my life are presently being diminished by guilt?

Money? Sex? Time? Children? Friends? Health? Work? Hobbies? Spiritual Growth? Dreams? Enthusiasm? Playfulness? Free time?

_____

_____

_____

_____

_____

_____

_____

_____

2. Which of the insights presented in this chapter could be helpful in dissolving this guilt?

_____

_____

_____

_____

_____

_____

_____

_____

The great news here is that the more you practice the concepts in this book, the better each of the areas listed above will become! As my life radically improved, I sometimes encountered individuals whose comments smacked of envy. I had to remind myself that I had had people feel sorry for me in the past, and that I would definitely rather be envied than pitied!

Now ask yourself:

- Would you harshly judge a child who was gifted in music or art?

- Would you try and hold back a child who was good at making friends?

- Would you be saddened or ashamed of a child who had all the time in the world to play and discover the world around them?

These questions take us back to this chapter's opening definition of innocence. Just as when we find ourselves going back to scarcity thoughts we can remind ourselves of abundance, so when we slip back into Am-I-guilty-thinking, we can gently remind ourselves of our perfection and innocence.

▶ MONEY GUILT

Probably the most challenging exercise is to carry a positive image of a child born into great wealth and feel happy for it. Literature and film are rife with examples of how wealth at an early age has been a curse to a child rather than a blessing. We obviously need a new set of pictures of happy children in wealthy families. Meanwhile, with these less positive pictures in our heads, we as adults must free ourselves to see any financial success we may have as a pure blessing rather than a mixed bag.

Guilt concerning money pervaded my thinking for the first 30 years of my life. I realized early in my business career that I had a habit of sabotaging my financial success whenever it started to look too promising. After all, during the late '60's I'd marched in Washington, D.C., carrying banners with messages about the evils of money and power!

To get beyond this limiting mindset, I pulled out Dr. Branden's exercise for exposing subconscious agendas and wrote, "The good thing about making less money is..." I was amazed as I continued to write, "...then no more children will starve in India." I was shocked, hardly believing I had written those words that were obviously buried deep inside me.

My particular 'button' for this happiness issue was my belief that there wasn't enough money to go around and that my having more would cause increased suffering in the world. Instant Guilt!

To get out of my guilt mentality, I had to create a new picture in my mind: A paradigm of abundance. By recalling that one out of every 100 people in this country is a millionaire, I reframed the situation. My extra income would come from all those millionaires' pocket change! I determined they would never miss it, and no one would have to suffer because of the abundance I acquired. As a result, the money I was ready to receive poured into my life.

Years later I dated a very wealthy business owner. At first I was put off by the expensive gifts and fancy restaurants. But as I fell in love with him, I saw that he was a wonderful next level of healing for my guilt about money. I watched him work hard for his money, be extremely generous to non-profits and individuals, and have to deal with those who wanted to be his friend primarily so that they could receive from his deep pockets.

I saw that having money does not in itself make life easier or harder. Our spiritual path is still inner work, not outer. My friend had as many challenges as I had. He could not buy his way into peace anymore than I could sing my way into it. He envied others for different aspects of life, just as they envied him for his wealth. The challenge before us is not first to gain more money, but first to overcome fear, envy and guilt and move into joy. Then the money, and all we desire, will flow.

In the area of money, my best antidote to those life-strangling emotions has been the 4 A's mentioned in the last chapter:

I am now *aware* of my money: everything from checking account balances to interest on loans and CD's. This gets me out of fear and disdain and helps me befriend this form of energy.

I now *accept* my responsibility for my income, realizing that I can have as high an income as I desire and am willing to allow into my life. When I become anxious about something that I don't have yet, I gratefully *accept* the perfection of the present moment, accepting that I am right where I need to be on my path and that my income simply mirrors my thinking. This gets me out of envy.

I now have more *accurate assessments* about money. I see those who have it and those who do not have it as no better or no worse than any others. My favorite people on the planet include the penniless and the well-positioned. I do not judge myself differently at different levels of income. This gets me out of guilt.

My *action* for dealing with money is to be in joy every moment as I continue to attract all that is good to myself.

▶ THE INACCURATE ASSESSMENT

A gentleman at one of my seminars asked this question. "I'm stuck at an income of $40,000. I feel like I've hit my own glass ceiling. Could I have a hidden agenda?"

I asked him to tell me every association he had with the number $40,000. "It's how much my Dad made," he told me. Within minutes we identified his inaccurate assessments about, "How much you make is how much you're worth."

Once he had separated his Dad's value from his Dad's income, he could continue to honor the former while surpassing the latter. He was able to free up his thinking and break open his 'ceiling' almost immediately.

Being happy is the most loving thing you will ever do for those who live with you or work with you. I once asked a group at a large corporation to write down ten things they could do to improve their attitudes at work. Before starting to write, one woman yelled, "The only thing I could do for my attitude at work is to *quit*!"

The man across the aisle from her said, "Now that would improve everyone's attitude!" Laughter broke out. Happiness and misery are both contagious.

▶ GUILT OVER A MISTAKE

Not only do we find ourselves guilty about being happy, but we push happiness away because we feel guilty about something we did or did not do in the past.

I was speaking to a group of homeless and recovering adults one morning when I asked them what they thought God thought of what they had done with their lives so far.

The answers were painful to hear. Under the perception of having let God down, self-condemnation was extreme! I asked the group to engage with me in a dialogue about parenting.

"For those of you who have had young children living in your home, do you recall a day when you realized it was time to warn your child about the dangers of a hot stove?"

They nodded.

"And how many of you gave such warnings, with demonstrations of where not to touch, and what would happen if they did?"

All the parents' hands went up.

"And after that, how many of your children still had a painful experience from touching the stove, despite your stern warnings?"

All the parents' hands went up again.

"And how many of you then, at that moment of their painful awareness, ran into the kitchen and spanked them for having disobeyed you?"

The room was still.

"And yet you're telling me that you believe that this loving God of yours punishes us at such times in our lives for disobeying the laws of the universe, rather than pouring out an abundance of comfort and love."

In the past few years a Unity teaching has helped me tremendously in this area:

We are not punished for our sins, we are punished by them.

► CONTAGIOUS MISERY

Let me conclude this section about guilt with a story of a 19-year-old GED student who came to me for help. "I don't know how to stay positive," he began. "It's easy at school, but when I get home, my Mom's always reminding me what a loser I am. Like yesterday, I forgot to take out the garbage, and she said that she was tired of throwing all her time and money away on somebody so worthless... What am I supposed to do with that?"

First, I reminded him of his need to protect himself against such poisonous, destructive criticism. He agreed and said he knew he needed to move out. Then I assured him that he was not the object of his mother's hatred . "Oh, I know it's herself she hates," he said. "She tells me about every other day she wishes she were dead."

This mother's misery was draining the joy from the life of her beloved son. Unhappiness is not only contagious, it can be deadly.

The world is as we are.
Ayurvedic Saying

▶ THE TRUTH SETS US FREE

We have all avoided happiness in one way or another throughout our lives. Therefore, in addition to acknowledging the four falsehoods in this chapter, we need to counter them with truths. Our affirmations might look like this:

▶ 1. Counteracting the fear of getting happiness:
I am open and welcoming to greater happiness and the changes it brings.

▶ 2. Counteracting the fear of losing happiness once we have it:
I cannot lose happiness. I am safe. Since I choose not to give anyone or any event the power to take my happiness and serenity away from me, I know that happiness is mine each day that I choose it. When what seems to be a loss occurs, I remember that the most important things in life have no end, and that the road to success is never a straight line.

▶ 3. Counteracting the belief that we do not deserve it:
Each day that I live, I remind myself of my worth and the worth of all living beings. Understanding that we are all Half-Jerk/Half-Jewel, I will honor my own gifts, own my weaknesses, and not put anyone above or beneath me. I know that happiness is a free gift that, rather than having to deserve, I may choose to invite into my life at any given time.

▶ 4. Counteracting the feelings of guilt:
I know there is abundant happiness. By choosing happiness, I am spreading it to those with whom I live, socialize, and work. This benefits myself and all those around me. When I remember who I am, I remember that I am innocent and perfect.

It is easy to see how we can and must change our minds and choices. Healing begins within, with letting the light of our joy, beauty, talents, and power shine forth.

Our deepest fear is not that we are powerless.
Our deepest fear is that we are powerful beyond measure.
It is our light, not our darkness that most frightens us.
We ask ourselves, who am I to be brilliant, gorgeous, talented, and fabulous?
Actually, who are you not to be? Your playing small doesn't serve the world.
There is nothing enlightened about shrinking
so that other people won't feel insecure around you.
And as we let our own light shine,
we unconsciously give other people permission to do the same.
As we are liberated from our fear,
our presence automatically liberates others.

Marianne Williamson

▶Practice Makes People

Once we accept that our happiness is not only good for us, but also good for the world, it's time to begin the process of determining what we can do immediately to be happier and healthier. There is no reason to wait until tomorrow to be happier when happiness is here for the asking today.

Before we begin this adventure of establishing which habit you want to focus on first, answer these simple questions:

1. How important is increasing your happiness to you at this time? (On a scale of 1–10)

_____

2. How much total time each day would you be willing to dedicate to being happier?

(Do not exaggerate here. If the answer is 30 seconds, write 30 seconds!) Maximum time = 60 minutes.

_____ minutes   _____ seconds

3. How willing are you to release old habits and risk trying something completely new? (On a scale of 1–10 with 10 being 100% willing)

_____

The definition of insanity is
doing what you've always done
and expecting a different result.

You have done the work, so far, of knowing what you don't want, and knowing what you do. Pick something physical in your environment (a rock, a calendar, a journal, a new piece of jewelry) to remind you each day of your intention of joy.

You have now programmed the amount and speed of change that will come into your life. Hang on!

The jump

is so frightening

between where

I am and

where I want to be...

because of all I may become

I will

close my eyes

and leap!

mary anne r. hershey

▶ EXERCISE

Imagine that today you received news that your workplace had changed its salary scale for the coming year. Starting next week, everyone will be paid, not by their skill level, education, or years of service, but based on their attitude for that week, as recorded by the 'attitude detectors' throughout the worksite. (Kirlean Photography for instance.)

The individuals with the most positive attitudes will get 'split-the-lottery' kinds of bonuses, while those with the most negative attitudes will get minimum wage with no benefits. Those in-between will receive salaries and benefits commensurate with their attitudes.

Now, write out your answers to the following:

1.   What would you do differently to earn the highest income? (List 20 or more things before continuing.)

_____

_____

_____

_____

_____

_____

_____

_____

_____

_____

_____

_____

_____

_____

_____

2.   What will keep others from earning a high salary?

_____

_____

3.   Who at your workplace will most likely start out at the highest salary? Why? Describe their behaviors.

_____

_____

_____

_____

_____

_____

After you complete the previous exercise, check back to the answers you gave to question 1 and ask: "How many of these behaviors take more than five minutes a day or cost more than $10 a week?" Usually it is very few. The attitude adjustments which we push to the end of our to-do list require neither time nor money. They only require commitment.

A positive attitude is not the result of magic fairy dust sprinkled on us at birth. It is the result of specific day-to-day behaviors. Positive attitudes occur in people who engage in positive, proactive behaviors.

No matter how positive or negative our attitude is at this moment, we can improve it with the 12 habits listed in the upcoming section. Taking the mystery out of attitude adjustment is one more step on the road to successful living.

> _What you and I will become in the end_
> _will be just more and more of what we are deciding_
> _and trying to be right now._
>
> John Powell, S.J.

►The Habits of Happiness

The following list of 12 happiness habits is in alphabetical order for easy reference. It is not meant to be comprehensive, but rather a list of basic factors that make the most noticeable and long-term differences in an individual's Score or Happiness Quotient (HQ).

Do some habits tend to make a greater difference in HQ than do others? Absolutely! You'll see that the chapters on the first four habits, A, B, C and D, are longer. They tend to be the heavy hitters as far as impact goes. Then there's my most recent favorite, G. You'll find you own favorites, just as I have.

Keep in mind that no one behavior is the key to a high HQ. All behaviors are ingredients. Some very happy people might only practice one or two of these behaviors on a regular basis. Others mix three or four into a given week. Your recipe for success will be unique to you, so find from the list what interests and motivates you, then make a commitment with your Coach to follow through.

▷ THE 12 HABITS OF HAPPINESS ◁

(A) Ask for what you want

(B) Be here now

(C) Change your thoughts

(D) Dream and imagine

(E) Expect a miracle

(F) Feel all your feelings

(G) Gratitude and appreciation

(H) Hugs and touch

(I) Insulate from the negative

(J) Journal

(K) Keep on keeping on

(L) Lighten up and laugh

Ask For What You Want (A)

Ask, and it shall be given...
Matthew 7:7

What would life be like if the above quote from Matthew were true? Too glorious to imagine? Magical? Boring? Well, it is true. In fact, it is one of the greatest truths. Yet it is one of the most misunderstood, certainly, for most of us do not understand that in moving from victim to volunteer, all we need to do is ask and then free ourselves to accept and allow for greater happiness.

So where do we begin in asking? Our first job is to face the four blocks discussed in the first section of this book. Once you've completed the exercises, take a deep breath. Remind yourself that you've been doing your best so far, but you're ready for better and willing to develop new habits in order to reach your goals. (It might be a good time to re-read your goals from page 8.)

Next, we need to learn to ask for what we want and stop asking for what we don't. The second part, learning how to clarify what we don't want so that we can refocus on what we do, is the difference between being those who are 'fine' and those who are 'fantastic'!

We have already learned that "as a man thinks, so he is." So it is important to remember that we ask in two ways, with our words and also with our thoughts. In this chapter, we will look at asking with words. In the chapter on habit C we will look at how to ask with our thoughts. Through both of these approaches we will better understand why some people seem to live 'charmed' lives when they are merely living in harmony with the universal laws.

▶ HOW TO ASK WITH WORDS (AND GET 90% OF WHAT YOU ASK FOR)

She was a beautiful woman in her mid-thirties. Her eyes were red from weeping as she walked toward me. After everyone else had left the seminar, she shared how a recent trip to Florida with her husband had rekindled her yearning to live near water. However, because of his job, they had lived in the Midwest for ten years.

"I stood on the boardwalk, crying like a baby. My husband reached out to me, but I gasped, 'I'm dying... we're dying... I've got to move back... I can't take it anymore.'"

I asked her how he responded. "He said he had noticed how peaceful I seemed there, that he hadn't seen me this happy since the last time we were in Florida."

Her husband saw that her request was not only a matter of preference, but a deeply felt need. When they returned home, they began working out a plan to get the family back to the coast.

This loving woman had been afraid to ask for what she needed for fear it would inconvenience her family. Yet her efforts to be unselfish could have threatened her health and her marriage.

Many of us have 'lived' in the same place. Having learned as children not to ask for a gift but let it be a surprise, we have dragged our feet through life hoping that someone would read our minds and give us what we want. Soon, we even forgot what we wanted. We only became acutely aware of what we *did not* want.

This is a chapter on how to identify our own needs and desires and express them lovingly. To desire is a very spiritual concept. De-sire means 'of the Father'. We cannot not desire. So this chapter will help us make our desiring more conscious.

> *Start where you are. You're at this moment standing*
> *in the middle of a great opportunity.*

When we vocalize our desires it lets those around us know more clearly who we are, and gives them a more complete picture with which to make their decisions. Not to do so can result in unnecessary pain.

In his best-selling book on marriage, *Getting the Love You Want,* Harville Hendrix says that it is extremely hard to get couples to ask for what they want, so he often asks them what they *don't* want. His advice includes these steps:

1. Identify something that makes you uncomfortable, a 'thorn' causing pain.

2. Isolate the desire behind the pain.

3. List a few do-able behaviors from your partner that would satisfy the desire.

These simple steps work not only in a marriage but in all of life. Just ask yourself: How much of what I *don't* ask for do I get? Probably not much. Now ask: How much of what I *do* ask for do I get? My personal experiences and data from others indicate that, in time and with a non-aggressive manner, we will get nearly 90% of what we ask for. It's a risk worth taking.

▶ WHY WE DON'T ASK

So why don't we ask? Here are some reasons and some suggestions:

1. **We aren't sure what we want.**   Get out a journal and write.
                                                    (See habit J)

2. **We believe our needs aren't valid.**   Affirm that you deserve happiness
                                                    and that allowing others to meet
                                                    your needs is part of life's
                                                    banquet. (See habit C)

3. **We still believe in scarcity:**   Reaffirm every day that life
   "There's not enough for me."   offers you abundance.

4. We believe, "If they really cared about me, I wouldn't have to ask."

Acknowledge your thinking pattern that is keeping you from allowing yourself to feel good. (See habit C)

5. We would feel personally rejected if someone told us, "No."

Realize the answer is about where they are at, not a personal affront to you, and continue to affirm that your answer is coming. (Reread pages 30–44 on risking)

6. We believe only weak people ask for what they want.

Remind yourself that studies show that the healthiest and wealthiest among us are those best at asking for help.

7. We fear getting it, thinking "What if things still don't improve? Or, "What if they do improve and I don't have any more excuses?"

Reaffirm your growing ability to welcome and embrace joy.

8. We don't know how to ask. In the past we've either come across as belligerent or whiney.

You simply need to learn how to ask. (Keep reading this chapter!)

Which do you regret more, the risks you didn't take or the risks you did?

▶ A Formula for Asking

Good communication occurs when the receiver receives the same message as was sent. If it sounds easy, guess again. We sometimes send a message about two or three things at once: "I'm upset with you about what you said today, but I'm really still angry about your not following through on your promise of yesterday," is often communicated as, "You can be so inconsiderate!"

The receiver is then left to unravel all the meanings. "What is she referring to/ What does she want/ Why is she attacking me?" If decoding seems too arduous a task, the receiver may simply give up and withdraw or end the exchange with an attack of their own.

An easier and more fruitful option is the use of a simple but powerful **4-step process.** This 'four-mula' clarifies for both parties what message is being sent, while avoiding judgments and helping us stick to the facts.

At first, the steps may seem awkward or too formal for regular use. However, many variations are possible. I use some form of these 4-steps practically every day. Once you become familiar with the process, you can develop your own style for saying the same thing in different ways.

Ask for What You Want (side tab)

Ⓐ ▶ How to Ask for What You Want

Pre-step: Have you got just a minute?

1. When _____ (event)

   happened at _____ (time and place)

2. I felt (a little) _____

   _____

3. because _____

   _____

4. Therefore, I would like you to consider OR therefore I am considering:

   _____

   _____

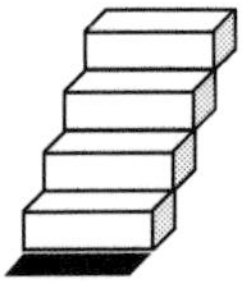

Pre-step: Asking for someone's attention in this multi-tasking world is absolutely vital. I have heard painful stories from those who tried to ask in the hallway while the other was leaving for work, or while the kids were interrupting, or during the last two minutes of the Super Bowl! Asking the other person to turn off all the other 'channels' to tune into yours is a must! If they say "no," simply ask when you could have a few minutes in the next 24 hours.

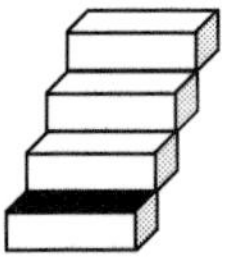

Step 1: List only one event that happened recently (preferably within 24 hours) with no exaggeration or judgment in your description.

A. **Usual:** "Why do you always leave everything right in front of the door..."

   Better: "When you came home from school today and left your books and jacket in front of the door ..."

B. **Usual:** "Since we *never* go on dates anymore..."

   Better: "When it's been over a month since we've been on a date..."

C. **Usual:** "When you said *last week* that you didn't care whether I went on the trip or not..." (Seven days ago is not recent enough for either of you to remember exactly what was said.)

   Better: "When you said at lunch today that you didn't care if I went on the trip or not..."

This is the most commonly abused section of the four-mula. In the heat of the moment, we want to lump all our grievances into one big bang. But if we 'win' an argument, no one wins. Stick to the most recent event. Your listener's chances of being able to 'hear' that they could have made a better choice *this one time* are a thousand times greater than if you drop a truckload of 'shoulds' and 'oughts' on their head all at once.

Step 2: State a feeling, not an opinion. Avoid "that," "like" and "as if."

A: **Usual:** I felt *that* you are being rude and careless...

　　Better: I felt a little upset and concerned...

B: **Usual:** "I feel *as if* you don't care anymore..."

　　Better: "I feel kind of disconnected and lonely..."

C. **Usual:** "I felt *like* you weren't being honest..."

　　Better: "I got this funny, uncomfortable feeling inside..."

Many times people begin *opinion* statements with "I feel," such as "I feel we should take another look at this." We do this because we know feelings are the most honest and open communication level and we want the other party to perceive us in that light. But when we start using opinions in "I feel" statements, it too often comes out as, "I feel that you just don't care," or "I feel like you are avoiding the issue...". Any such statements are sure to build huge walls and keep us from attaining our goals. By simply adding the phrase "a little" after "I feel," the problem is solved. We will never say, "I feel a little that you don't care." But we might say, "I feel a little upset and concerned." We automatically remind ourselves to stay out of assuming or judging and stay with the most powerful level of communication: feelings. However, some people get defensive at the suggestion of using "a little."

"A little? No way! I am really ticked off..."

Okay, time for a deep breath.

Do you remember the first time this action upset you? The very first time, you weren't that upset. But for whatever reason, (see previous list) you didn't say anything at the time. You waited, and the problem got worse. Except to them, it's not a problem. They don't realize how much this is bothering you. So, share the 'news' that it is bothering you 'a little' at a time.

Step 3: Share why you feel as you do *without judging.*

A: **Usual:** "Because you're 17 years old but you obviously haven't learned the skills of living with other people..."

　　Better: "Because I believe part of my job as your parent is to teach you how to share living space..."

B. **Usual:** "Because you never care enough to..."

　　Better: "Because our dates are important to me..."

C: **Usual:** "Because you have a tendency to hold things in..."

　　Better: "Because I wondered if you were still upset about last year's trip..."

Ask for What You Want

Although the word 'you' is often necessary in Step 1 of the four-mula, it is not the focus of Step 3. This is your chance to explain the thoughts behind your emotional reaction. Don't assume they understand where you're coming from. Tell them. *Then ask them what they heard you say.*

Step 4: When it feels appropriate, paint a word-picture of what specific actions could be taken to improve the situation, or describe a future action you are considering taking if things don't improve. (It is very important here not to exaggerate or nag, or threaten an action without following through.)

A: **Usual:** "Don't ever leave things lying around again. I'm warning you!"

    Better: "Therefore, if it happens again, I'll simply put the items in a safe, locked place, and you'll have to buy them back for five dollars an item."

B: **Usual:** "If you want this marriage to survive, some things better change!"

    Better: *Woman:* "So, I'd like you to ask me out some time in the next week. I'd love it if you'd choose where we go, what we do, get the sitter, the works. Thanks for listening!"

    Man: "So, I am asking you on a date this Friday night. I already have the sitter... etc."

Pick something that you want to ask someone for and use the four-mula above to write out what you would like to say:

Pre-step: Have you got a minute?

1. When

_____

_____

2. I felt (a little)

_____

_____

3. because

_____

_____

4. Therefore

_____

_____

For couples only:

For those in long-term relationships, there is another, more in-depth fourmula:

1. When

_____

_____

2. it triggered in me some feelings of

_____

_____

3. which made me concerned/scared that

_____

_____

4. Therefore, I would appreciate it if you would

_____

_____

This week, ask for one thing that you want. See it as an experiment rather than attaching any deep meaning to it. If you feel a need for support, set up a time for each 'asking' on your appointments calendar. Call your Coach before your request to get moral support. Call again once you have completed your asking to celebrate your courage.

As the weeks progress, answer these questions concerning your requests: How do I feel while asking? After asking? How do people respond? Do things seem to be improving when I ask for what I need? Do I feel a need for more coaching in this skill?

_____

_____

_____

_____

_____

Ask for What You Want

▶ DESTRUCTIVE VS. CONSTRUCTIVE CRITICISM

Using these 4 steps will elimininate (the bulldog of) destructive criticism. "How come you always have to write your book and Dad is never home and Jo always gets to play with the dog!?!" These words from my 9-year-old were indications that Zach's inner-bulldog was awake. The bulldog is that part of us that does destructive criticism.

We'll talk about how to get out of the bulldog in the chapter on Habit F, but for now you should know that NO progress will be made until the one doing the destructive criticism can calm down enough to move into a more positive, constructive mode.

Destructive criticism happens when we criticize someone's *character*. The words coming out of our mouths in Step 1 sound like, "You always" or, "You never" or name calling like, "You are such a...." I remember a time when I had been in a new relationship for just a few months when he said, "Sometimes I'm not comfortable with the way you parent your teenager." Well, a bulldozer would have been gentler.

Constructive criticism is when we confront *one behavior*. In order to ask for what we want and get it, we must be in control of our thoughts and feelings enough to be constructive. When others use destructive criticism against us, we simply need to ask them to rephrase a generalization into a specific thing we did recently to upset them.

If someone chooses not to rephrase a destructive comment, they are most likely in a bulldog mode, and are not really interested in solving, just in venting. If they are willing to use the 4 steps to rephrase their request to be more specific and non-judgmental, you will usually find yourself most willing to hear them out.

▶ WHY CHANCE IT?

There are many good reasons to ask for what we want. We feel better, more connected with others. We learn about and validate ourselves by expressing our needs to others. Meanwhile, one of the best reasons for asking is that when we get what we ask for, everyone benefits.

▶ THE FRESHMAN AND THE PROFESSOR

When I was a freshman at a state university in the '70's, it was not uncommon to have 500 to 1000 students in each classroom. This severely limited the interaction between students and professors, making it extremely difficult to ask questions.

At one lecture midway through the first semester, our professor was describing a writer this way; "Of course, he believed in God, and we all know that is the great delusion."

Something inside me snapped. I raised my hand in the huge lecture hall and was ignored. I stood and waved my hand and was ignored. I finally made my way into the aisle and started down front to where the professor was lecturing.

As I headed toward him, he finally acknowledged me. "Yes, Miss. May I help you?" he asked coolly.

"I hope so, Professor. Will the statement about belief in God as 'the great delusion' be on the mid-term, or is it just your personal opinion?" After a slight pause, he stated it would not be included on the exam.

I believe, as did many of my classmates, that I helped not only myself and my class by expressing my concern, but potentially also the individual I confronted.

Asking for what we want is essential for a balanced and happy life. Like the woman who needed to be near the ocean in the first story of this section, our needs cannot be shoved aside. Not asking for what we want is usually more selfish than asking for it. Our misery makes others pay a high price for our silence.

There is another important reason we must learn to ask for what we need. Until we learn to ask, we will not trust that our needs will be met. There can be no intimacy without trust. Asking for what we need from another is an important step in building a healthy relationship. Only when we learn to ask will we have the reminders that we are safe and that we are cared for.

▶ THE GIFT OF ALLOWING

The ability to receive is as important as the ability to give. Like the blood that goes out of our arteries and into our veins, there must be a flow. Many times in my life I have found that I was anemic because I wasn't asking and/or allowing others to support me. Now I understand that the more I ask, the more I will receive. People want to give of their gifts. It is affirming to them.

I am reminded of a story from one of my seminar participants, a mother of three:

"My first two children were raised entirely by me until they were three years old. My husband had made it clear before we married that he didn't do diapers, feedings or potty training. Well, our third child was four months old when I fell and broke my hip. We had a talk about bringing someone in, but I asked him to rethink his rules. He did and began parenting our baby that evening. The transformation in him and in our family was absolutely a miracle."

▶ SETTING OUR LIMITS

It is important to know which limits we can bend while staying true to ourselves and which we cannot. I had years of binge eating in my 20's and early 30's, and food is an area that still requires my heightened awareness. Before a recent visit to family members, I called to let them know that I was eating lower-fat foods than the last time they had seen me. "So I would really appreciate if everyone focused on their own food choices and allowed me to make mine while I'm there."

In the past, such a call might have upset them, but we have all grown. Before other visits, I have requested such things as limits on smoking indoors, or the amount of time the television was on. My visits are now more frequent and longer in duration because I have risked making these requests.

Asking is such a simple thing. It not only prevents problems from either beginning or getting worse, it also heightens everyone's awareness, so there are fewer guessing games in life.

A   ► **HEARING "NO," SAYING "NO"**

Ask for What You Want

The final step to successful asking is to let go of the outcome. If we do not get what we want from the other party, we simply move on to get our needs met elsewhere. For example, in the example about my family mentioned above, I can always bring my own food, stay at a hotel, or shorten my stay if visiting becomes unpleasant.

If we have not yet learned to let go of the outcome, chances are that we are not receiving honest responses because people are afraid to tell us the truth. The process of asking is often much more important, much more life-giving, than how or when or by whom our needs are answered. When we have communicated our needs in a respectful manner, others have a better understanding of us, and their response has given us a better understanding of them.

To encourage individuals to give me their truest answers even though a "no" might be painful, I sometimes begin a request with a simple introduction such as this one: "I'm going to ask you a favor in a minute. I will be fine with either a yes or no answer. If this doesn't work for you, you don't need to even tell me why you need to decline. I really want to find someone who feels completely comfortable with saying yes. You can think about it and call and leave your answer on my machine anytime in the next 24 hours. Thanks! Now, my request is..."

One wonderful thing about people saying "no" to us is that it reminds us that we can say "no" as well! My favorite version is, *"No, I won't be doing that, but thank you for asking!"* Each of us has limits and boundaries, and saying "no" is simply admitting that to the other party. Saying "no" is sometimes more difficult than receiving it as a response. But if we do not say an honest "no" today, the truth of our real feelings will be more painful tomorrow.

The best thing for me to do when I am asked for an immediate answer that I am unsure of is to let them know I'll get back with them in 24 hours. Then I am almost always able to find peace in my answer either way.

> *Plain "Yes" or "No" is all you need to say.*   Matthew 5:37

Asking is simple but not always easy. Which of the following gifts would most help you to ask for what you want?

1. A friend to be there with me while I make the phone call.

2. A friend to encourage me before I ask and then be there as a safety net for after I ask.

3. Reading this chapter over and practicing the fourmula in front of a mirror.

4. Reading a book on this subject such as, "The Aladdin Factor" by Jack Canfield.

5. Things getting even worse than they are now, forcing me to ask.

(In reality, if you don't ask now, #5 will come to pass!)

▶ ASK WITH HOPE (AND GET 99% OF EVERYTHING YOU ASK FOR)

In order to raise your success rate in receiving what you ask for, you must believe you will receive it. Okay, I hear you, "But how do I start to believe if I don't now?" A belief is a thought that is repeated over and over and over. When doubts or fears come up, simply release them with, "*No, I won't be going there, but thank you for sharing.*" Visualize as close to the perfect outcome as you can until you start to feel better. Let's do an example:

"I want a raise of $10,000 a year."

This is not hard for God/the Universe, or whatever is your name for The Source. The only thing stopping you from that raise is your thought/belief pattern. If you follow that thought with "but I know I'll never get it," you are correct, you never will.

If you think you can or you think you can't, you're right.

Henry Ford

Go to the next best thought: "I will get a $5000 raise because I really deserve it." Can you believe this? Picture the scene in your mind. Pretend, imagine, visualize, draw, daydream, cut out pictures, role-play. Whatever you can do to bring this picture fully into your senses will help it manifest more quickly.

▶ RELEASE THE OUTCOME

I often hear hesitation... "But what if I don't get it?" So? Is your fear of loss so great that you think you could not live with the answer? If this person says 'no', they are not saying 'no' to your request, they are saying, "No, I'm not the one who is to fulfill your request, so keep looking, your request WILL be granted!" In addition, when the answer is "Yes," which it usually is, we are happier. Asking is key to reaching our goals and living an exciting, joy-filled life.

A CEO who heard me speak on this subject years ago came up to me after the seminar. "I so appreciate your sharing," he began. "Three people turned in their resignations last week. During the exit interviews they shared why they were leaving — what was missing from their experience here. In all three cases I would have given them what they asked in a heartbeat. But they never asked."

If you don't ask, you don't get.

Ghandi

▶ A COUPLE OF FINAL POINTS...

Sometimes with close friends or spouses, it's helpful to use numbers to convey what level of discomfort you're feeling. With a girlfriend I might leave a message to give me a call and end with: "It's only a 2!" Note that if you're leaving a lot of "10" messages, your life is trying to tell you something!

I discovered years ago, however, that even numbers can mean different things to different people. I once told my partner that something was "just a 3." He radically changed that something the next day. When I asked him about the sudden shift, he said, "I hate to have 3's. Anything over a 2 is major to me!"

From time to time when I've made a request, I am asked why I didn't tell them about it a long time before. I simply answer that I had just allowed myself to become aware of it, so I couldn't tell them any sooner.

Okay, that's it. Now it's your turn. Practice asking at least a couple of times a week. Trust the process. As your coach, I guarantee this method, when "taken as directed," is 90–100% successful! Have fun getting what you want!

> *The world is so full of a number of things,*
> *I'm sure we should all be as happy as kings!*

> Robert Louis Stevenson

Be Here Now (B)

Enjoy today: this is not a dress rehearsal.

Refrigerator magnet

The 'Be Here Now' habit sounds so simple and so obvious. Where else would I be? And yet in today's society the individual who is living most of his or her life in the present is rare. The good news is that we can all come home to presence in the blink of an I.

Being Here Now couldn't be simpler. Or more challenging. There are three components to living in the present. It's as easy as ABC, only it's FGH.

(F) Getting our focus out of the past through Forgiveness

Unplugging from:

- Regret — "I should have..."
- Bitterness — "They should have..."
- Nostalgia — "The good old days..."

(G) Fully experiencing the moment through Gratitude

- Going GA GA with gratitude and appreciation
- Experiencing being beyond thought

(H) Getting our focus off of the future through Hope

Unplugging from

- Fear: "What if I..."
- Worry: "What if they..."
- Putting Joy on Hold: "I'll be happy when..."

For our discussion here, we will use the concepts of focus, energy and thought interchangeably. As the adage goes, "Where thought goes, energy flows." Just as each of us has only so much energy at a given time, so we have a finite number of thoughts. According to author Caroline Myss, when our energy or thought 'circuits' are tied up in either the past or the future, we have nothing left for this moment. Before we even walk out the door to head for work, we can be depleted and drained.

In Thornton Wilder's play, *Our Town,* the main character, Emily, goes back in time to relive a childhood birthday party, only to find presents but no *presence*. Everyone did things for Emily, but no one stopped to relate to her, to just be with her. These human beings had fallen into the trap of becoming 'human doings'. The good news is that we can learn to pull our focus out from the past and the future and be completely present to each other and to ourselves, one thought at a time.

▶ THE FGH FORMULA

A simple way to think ourselves into the greatest happiness and peace that life has to offer is return each moment to FGH:

Ⓕ Forgiveness of the past,

Ⓖ Gratitude for the present

Ⓗ Hope for the future.

"But I have thousands of thoughts!" Yes, you do, but every one of them is either about the past, present, or future. To transform a thought into F, G or H, we just catch it like a firefly! Once we 'hear ourselves' thinking a thought, then, like the old telephone operators saying, "Just a moment, I'll connect you...," we can plug into a new thought.

The exciting news for those of us who are on this path is that we can tell whether we are present by recognizing whether or not we are conscious of our thoughts. The moment we realize "I am not present," I *am* present! When we can learn to observe our thoughts, we are halfway home to redirecting them or releasing them altogether.

▶ GETTING OUT OF THE PAST

The first area where we need to become conscious is the amazing amount of our thoughts that are stuck in the mud of yesterday. Somewhere along the way, we picked up a belief that rehashing what *has been* will make us safer or healthier, or that we have to share all of our childhood wounds with each other in the name of 'openness and honesty'.

Yet, if we were completely honest, we would limit ourselves to acknowledging only the best of who we are, for, *honestly*, that is our true essence. Any memory that causes us pain is rehearsing a time when we were out of the flow of our natural beauty and innocence. The child who comes into the world pure never loses that purity, except in the minds of those who see the past with regret and bitterness.

The remedy for such stuckness is to free our energy and our love through a simple decision to forgive.

▶ A FATHER'S GIFT

In January the physician informed my father that he had an aggressive form of cancer. He lived in Florida and since neither I nor any of my four siblings lived there, we decided to alternate weeks so that one of us would be with him at all times.

It was six weeks later, my week with him, that I was at his hospital bedside for a profound experience. That afternoon, as he was recovering from a radiation treatment, he began to cough and choke. The nurse came in three times within an hour, but we all soon realized there was little she could do. The next time Dad started coughing I decided just to hold him. It seemed to last forever, and my tears of helplessness dripped onto his face. When at last the coughing let up, he looked up at me and asked, "Am I going to die today?"

I hesitated.

"I'm not sure, Dad. I don't know much about cancer, but I do know this, if you need to go today, you are ready." Just then the phone rang. It was my brother from Seattle. When I held the phone up to Dad's ear, all he could get out was a raspy, "I love you, I love you, I love you, I love you."

Miraculously, the phone kept ringing, as though everyone heard his pain and wanted to be there with him. His message for each was the same, "I love you, I love you, I love you, I love you." But there was one call that did not come, and I knew it was a call I had to make. I dialed the number and once more held the receiver to Dad's ear. "One more. You can do it, Dad."

The two had not spoken in some time. Dad's message was choked out between sobs, "I'm so sorry, I'm so sorry. Please forgive me, please forgive me..."

When I hung up the phone, he looked at me and asked, "Why did you do that?"

"Oh, Dad, you remember Jacob Marley from *A Christmas Carol*. You don't need those old chains to drag around. Where you're going, you want to go free."

And he did go free a few weeks later.

The chains of unforgiveness drag us down not only in the hereafter, but in the here and now. Those who desire the freedom of happiness cannot afford to be bound by them.

▶ LIFE IS FOR GIVING AND FOR GETTING

Do your best to imagine a world where we give no power to the past, where each moment is fresh and new. Such a notion transports us into almost an idyllic Garden of Eden, and yet it is available to us at any moment. Our, "Beam me up Scotty," magic words are simply, "I forgive you. Please forgive me."

"Why should I ask their forgiveness? I didn't do anything..." Anything is better than spending a part of your life judging them. And whether or not they forgive us, the biggest challenge is forgiving ourselves.

▶ THE REAL IN-A-ME

Think back to an event where you regret your behavior. Now ask yourself: "If I had known then what I know now, would I have done things differently?" When I pose the question in my workshops, the answer is almost always, "Yes." Therefore, it was not a matter of your being a bad person then and a good person now. *You did the best you could at the time with the information you had.* So did the other people you are having trouble forgiving.

Every time I find myself wallowing in bitterness ("they should have") or regret ("I should have"), I repeat the phrase, "We were all doing the best we could at the time with the information we had." This is extremely freeing. I come back to the here and now. I do my best and let go of the rest. I trust in a Higher Order to take care of any messes I made because I believe that all things work for good.

One secret of a long and fruitful life is to forgive everybody, everything, every night before you go to bed.

Ann Landers

Another form of not forgiving ourselves is to live in the past through nostalgia. "How I/we screwed up the 'good old days'" can be another way of keeping our energy frozen in

Be Here Now

another place and time. As a friend once remarked, "Nostalgia ain't what it used to be!" Comparing today to a glorified yesterday and coming up short is nothing but one more excuse to live in the past. To be ungrateful is to be not fully present, just as it is if we are not forgiving.

One day I realized that the only enemy I have is "in-a-me"

▶ HOW TO BE GRATEFUL FOR THE PAST

So how can we be grateful for obvious 'wrongs'? By acknowledging that life is always more than it seems to be on the surface.

My daughter was 13 when we discovered she had a stalker. She had thought at first that the nice man waving at her on her way to school was the assistant pastor of our parish. The dark hair and beard, along with the glasses and older car were similar for both.

When she realized it was not the priest, we reported it. The police decided it was perilous enough to warrant a stake out, and he was apprehended with a gun in his pocket on his next attempt to speak to her.

So, readers, do you have the big bad monster pegged yet? I did. I wanted nothing but his incarceration. The day of the hearing my daughter stayed home and I went to meet the man of whom we had lived in terror for three weeks, and later identified in a line-up.

After the official business of setting the charges was completed, the courtroom began to clear. I noticed an older couple speaking with his attorney. Five minutes later as they headed for the door, I walked up to them and introduced myself, saying my daughter and I intended him no harm. The woman began to cry while her husband tried to comfort her. "We are so sorry," she began. "We had no idea... please forgive him, please forgive us."

The story that followed, of a lonely man who had cared for years for his elderly parents and then been thrown into depression at their deaths, explained much.

My daughter had a high Score. He had a low one. He was looking for light and in her he had found it. He carried a gun out of fear of an unsafe world.

Not long afterwards I was able to help in getting his charges reduced from felony to misdemeanor and he is doing well today. I am so grateful... for everything. I can sincerely say the entire incident was a blessing.

▶ WHOSE DEBT IS LARGER?

In one of my seminars a woman was so angry about her brother-in-law not repaying an old $300 debt that I wanted to write her a check. But that, of course, would not have resolved 'the moral of the thing' that she claimed was holding her back from greater happiness.

I invited her to see this as an opportunity to learn the life lesson of forgiveness for a relatively inexpensive price. I know of individuals who have forgiven their family member's murderer. Forgiveness is not something anyone earns, it is a free gift. What surprises many people is that one who receives the greatest gift is the one who forgives.

Unforgiveness is like taking poison and hoping the other person will die!
"Taking Care of Me" Seminar Participant

▶ FORGIVING SELF

Often in life, we will never know why 'they' did what they did. But if we look back on why we did what *we* did, we can always see that somewhere along the line, our intention was love. So was theirs. I remember a woman, a mother of two, having a terrible time at 45 forgiving herself for an abortion she had at 15. I asked her to remind herself that she was doing the best she could at the time.

"But my Mom would have killed me!" she wailed. Later in our conversation she blurted out, "It would have killed her. It would have just killed her!" The young woman made a very pro-life decision based on love.

▶ REASSESSING REGRET

One December a few years back, I discovered that I had been ignoring a part of my business that was accruing debt. By the time I discovered it, it was such a huge sum that I closed our office downtown and moved it back to my home. For almost a month I was in shock and pain. How could I have closed my eyes so tight for so long?

Forgiving myself was slow at first. I simply walked around in circles feeling like a 'failure'. One day someone handed me a book and said, "Do what this book suggests and you will turn this around in no time." The book gave me a process for healing the wound. Within 24 hours I had hope again. Within 48 hours I felt grateful for the whole experience and for the fact that I caught it when I did. My forgiveness was intertwined with all of this and was complete within a week of my turning my thinking around to positive FGH thoughts.

When catching a glimpse of what could be is blinded by what was,
you've become 'historical'.

Glenn Van Ekeren, author of *12 Simple Secrets of Happiness*

▶ A MOTHER'S GUILT

I cannot complete this section without sharing a powerful forgiveness discussion with a young mother. After a seminar, she came up to me red-eyed and waited until everyone had left to begin our conversation.

"Tomorrow is the anniversary," she said, almost angrily. "If I had put a seat belt on my two year old, he would be alive today." I hugged her and said, "Or he wouldn't be, we will never know. What I do know is that you want me to join you in judging you as a bad mother. I will give you my answer after you hear my story...."

"Joanna was about 9 months old, and loved wheeling around the house in her walker. That day, unbeknownst to me, the door that went to our refrigerator pantry and eventually to our basement was not completely latched shut. Jo saw it, and her chubby little hands were able to quietly pry the door open while I was putting dishes in the dishwasher. I heard a cry and turned to see her walker heading down two steps to a landing. When I got to my crying baby, the wheels of the walker were an inch from the edge of the stairway that would have taken her down 10 more steps to a cement basement floor. "

"I'll give you my verdict as soon as you give me yours," I told the mother, who simply sobbed in my arms.

This next exercise will take you about 10 minutes. It is an accounting of those people in your life whom you have not forgiven. You have fully forgiven someone when you rejoice in their good fortune and feel compassion for their misfortune. If you take the allotted time to complete it, the list will surprise you. **Awareness of just how long and how old this list is will be a huge step forward in your ability to allow happiness into your life.** Use this checklist to determine whether you have been spending your life energy on the past. Then ask yourself how much energy/attention you have given to each.

Note: If you would feel more comfortable writing this on a separate sheet of paper and then burning or destroying it when you're finished, then do so!

1. Whom have I not forgiven and why?

_____

_____

_____

_____

_____

_____

_____

_____

_____

2. What have I not forgiven myself for?

_____

_____

_____

_____

_____

_____

3. Are there any other events from my past which I am bitter about?

_____

_____

_____

_____

_____

_____

_____

4. What parts of my past seemed ideal, so it is difficult to imagine ever matching their joy?

_____

_____

_____

_____

5. What percentage of my thoughts are still in the past at this point in my life? (0–100%)

_____

B

Be Here Now

You are at the top when you have made friends with your past,
you are focused on the present and optimistic about your future.

Zig Ziglar

▶ IS YOUR POWER IN YOUR PAST?

When we make friends with our past, even the part we know we may never understand, that friendship can bless us with greater focus, energy and clarity.

One high school student I'll call Kathy had lost her boyfriend in a car accident the previous year. One day near the end of our class sessions, she darted out of the room for no apparent reason. At the next class we heard her story.

It was raining. Not hard, just a light rain. But I was glad. That meant no one else would be at the cemetery. I went to his gravesite. I just stood there crying for awhile, then I said that I had come to take my power back. I promised I'd never forget him, but said I needed to let go and move on. I knew he would have wanted that for me... It felt really cleansing.

That young woman went on to become president of her senior class and continues to amaze me with her wisdom and courage.

▶ GETTING OUT OF THE FUTURE

Living in the future is just as detrimental as living in the past. As mentioned earlier, we have control over less than 1% of what we worry about. Yet worrying has become a national pastime, and is highly accepted and usually expected in most families, social groupings, and work places. When we find ourselves spending mental energy on something in the future, we can remind ourselves that F.E.A.R. is only False Evidence Appearing Real.

He who fears he shall suffer, already suffers what he fears.

Michel de Montaigne

Take five minutes to do Nathaniel Branden's exercise by completing the following phrases 3 times. Just write whatever comes to mind, no matter how illogical or irrelevant it may seem. If you get stuck with an "I can't think of anything else" thought, simply go to, "If I could think of another answer, what would it be?"

1. The good thing about **worrying about everybody else** all the time is:

_____

_____

_____

2. The good thing about **being too busy** all the time is:

_____

_____

_____

Congratulations! You can feel very good about trusting yourself and honoring yourself enough to complete this powerful exercise! Chances are your insights are enough right now, but if you'd like some of mine, the following are some of realizations I have come to over time:

1. **Worry:** I thought my reason for worrying was to figure things out, but I now understand that the hidden reason that I worry about others all the time is so that I don't have to worry about myself, look at my issues, or feel the feelings they will stir up in me! Worry keeps me from being present to the truth and gifts of this moment!

    In reality, I can never run away from myself. It's like a puppy trying to run from it's tail. The only peace comes in facing my issues and challenges. When I start to address my own issues, my obsessive worrying about others will cease.

2. **Busyness:** I thought my reason for being busy all the time was just that I had a lot of interests and a lot of things to accomplish! Now I see that the hidden reason why I was busy all the time was to avoid the risks of intimacy with my family, as well as the fear of being alone with myself and facing my Higher Power. I also used being busy as a con to convince myself and the rest of the world that I was 'somebody' when actually it was because I was feeling like a nobody.

    The truth for me is that only in embracing myself, my family, and the God that is 'closer than hands and feet' that I will find peace and joy. As I grow in serenity and happiness, the need for doing is replaced by a lust for being, and amazingly, the money still flows in, the kids are still well dressed and happy, the church choir somehow survives, etc....

> *My life has been a series of endless crises,*
> *most of which never happened.*
>
> Mark Twain

▶ I'LL BE HAPPY WHEN...

Another common form of living in the future is putting joy on hold. I remember thinking that I would be happy once I got into a committed relationship with a man. What I was failing to acknowledge was that I was in half a dozen close friendships with men and women at the time. Each friendship was special and unique. Each had commitments such as: honesty, openness, respect, equality, making time for each other, etc.

We never have to wait to do the 'stuff' of relationships. How we are doing our relationships right now is how we will do them in the future. If you don't have the energy to date now, you wouldn't have the energy to mate either. Meanwhile, there is really no such thing as waiting for a 'life partner'. When we release the element of time, (all relationships end on one level and on another level none of them end) there is only a 'this moment partner'.

> *The longer I live, the more romantic my friendships become*
> *and the more friendly my romances become.*
>
> Marianne Williamson

"Be Here Now" does not mean that we cannot hope for things to be different in the future. It means we can set our intentions for our next event and then release them, and see what is right now. This skill is not calling us to a life of instant gratification, but rather to living life one day at a time. We never know when it may be our last on this planet.

When we see something only as what it's going to become, we miss out on its presence in the moment. Having taught high school for 10 years, this has become evident to me. Many of us look at teenagers only as who they will become at some point. I remember the motivational speaker who came to the school where I was teaching. He walked in with the number of students written on a sheet of paper.

He announced the number, and then said, "Four of you will never make it to graduation. This is all you've got. Make it good."

When I am asked to sing at funerals, I often hear in the eulogy that the deceased was just beginning his retirement years. Statistics show that many retiring men make their transition within the following two years. The minister at these ceremonies often notes with regret that the deceased never realized what he had waited so long for. We cannot afford to wait until tomorrow to find joy.

▶ How to Be in the Moment

Here is a simple technique to find out if you are living in the present. Sit quietly each morning or evening and take 5 deep breaths. During this time, do your best to focus only on your breathing. When other thoughts come up, simply release them with a "thank you, not now." When you are finished, ask yourself: Where did my thoughts go? You will discover that many of them are rehearsing future events. It's good to be prepared. It's not good to be preoccupied.

Use this checklist to determine whether you have been spending your life energy on the future. Then ask yourself how much energy/attention you have given to each. Rate them 1–10, with 10 being for the most energy/attention.

How much energy am I giving to fears about financial security for myself or my family?

How much energy am I giving to, "What will they think if I...?" or "How do I look?"

How much do I think about loneliness or losing my close relationships?

To what extent do I feel concern about keeping my job, my clients, or my title?

How much do I worry about what will happen to others?

We do not know what tomorrow brings, but we know what we must do to be fully alive today. Life does not give us a headlight so that we can see the future results of our actions. It gives us a flashlight, so that we can see where we need to take our next step. When we do the best we can do one moment at a time, our long-term goals are realized.

Don't Worry, Be Happy.

▶ MINDFULNESS AND MODERN LIVING

One obvious sign of living in the Now, rather than in the future, is a slower pace and a less-driven life-style. We do not enjoy anything we rush to get done, yet hurrying is the normal pace in modern society. The antidote to rushing through life is mindfulness, being present to the moment and aware of what is going on within and around us.

"Take five" used to mean, "Take a five-minute break." Today, there is almost no one who actually gives themselves a break from working or worrying for five minutes. Even smokers spend most of their time 'fuming'. So, I propose we all start getting good at Taking Five Seconds. Next time you're in a meeting and tempers begin to flare, hold up five fingers nice and wide and remind everyone to breathe. It's a powerful reminder to your body and your mind that All Is Well.

Sign seen on retreat center bulletin board:

Things To Do Today: Inhale, Exhale, Inhale, Exhale, etc.

One of my mindfulness memories occurred one evening while I was out of town on a speaking engagement. Since the weather was inclement, my two choices for the evening meal were to go down to the dining room or eat dinner in my hotel room. I strayed from my norm and requested a meal be delivered to me in my room for the sole purpose of eating mindfully.

When the meal arrived, I quietly sat and took in all of its aroma and beauty. I said a prayer of thanks for those who had grown and prepared the food, as well as to the One who created the growers and preparers. Then I took a bite, and while chewing, focused all my attention on tasting it.

The above paragraph is not great literature, but it was a great meal! I had no conversations, responsibilities, or distractions from the simple and beautiful act of eating. I became painfully aware of how seldom I tasted my food, and wondered if I was more consumed by my daily activities than I was savoring them.

▶ VACATION EYES

One of my favorite mindfulness exercises is to see my world with what I call 'Vacation Eyes'. I pretend, as I'm driving home from the store, that I've never seen the street I'm on before. One day I'm in St. Louis, the next in Boston or Paris. The immediate feeling of awe and wakefulness is refreshing. I can do the same with everything, such as:

Pretending my ride up the elevator is my first ever

Pretending the meal I just cooked was prepared at a fancy restaurant

Pretending I was just hired, and it's my first day at work.

My other favorite Now-Game is to imagine that *this* moment is the moment I've been waiting for all my life. When? Right *now*. And then I have to guess why. It's a blast!

Remember, Being Here Now means celebrating each moment as a first time experience because you've never been *here now* before. Life is brand new in each moment, awaiting our discovery of its presents.

> *Normal day, let me be aware of the treasure you are. Let me learn from you, love you, bless you before you depart. Let me not pass you by in quest of some rare and perfect tomorrow. Let me hold you while I may, for it may not always be so. One day I shall bury my face in the pillow or stretch myself taut or raise my hands to the sky and want more than all the world your return.*
>
> Mary Jean Iron

▶ "SORRY, I'M NOT HERE RIGHT NOW"

Many an answering machine recording begins with the message, "Sorry, I'm not here right now." It reminds me of the postcard for business-driven vacationers: "Beautiful scenery. Amazing views. Wish I was here."

A happy and full life demands presence. I remember a time when I was sitting by a beautiful lake in Colorado. Suddenly I heard a car screech to a stop on the rocky road behind me. I looked over to see the driver and his companion jump out just long enough to snap a photograph, then jump back into the car and drive to their next mountain-top experience.

Similarly, I have sung with many accompanists who hurry through their piano solos to get to 'the important part' where the singer comes in. As a dancer, my daughter is learning the importance of completely finishing one movement before beginning the next.

The shortest way to do many things is to do only one thing at once.

Samuel Smiles

▶ Now Here This

The gentleman had just heard the speaker talk about presence. "I can't wait to get home to my kids and be present to them!" he said, and then laughed as he heard what he was saying. I know I've fallen into the trap of thinking I can be present somewhere else easier than here because here is boring, here is scary, here is negative, here is....

How you are going to be then and there is how you are being right here and now. We can only be present in the present moment.

"Be Here Now" behavior requires us to live each moment as if it were our last. When I feel I am losing this wonder-fullness, I take a deep breath, or meditate, or go barefoot and feel the grass under my feet, or spend some time with a child. I know that if I can become as engrossed in where I am right now as a little one is, I can reconnect with bliss, freedom, and the Now.

The hit movie *Hook* teaches us that if we lose all our todays for the long-term goals of tomorrow, we can forever become *hooked* into other than our top priorities.

At the 1996 Olympic Games, the father of a silver medalist swimmer who had been coaching his son for 17 years said, "I would love to take him fishing now. It will mean everything to me." Perhaps even more than an Olympic medal.

▶ The Solution to Every Problem

Eckhart Tolle once asked a small group of us, "Would you like the solution to all of your problems right now?" When we answered enthusiastically, he pointed out, "You have no problem right now. All of your problems are either in the future or the past. There is never a problem right now."

The Kingdom is at hand. Mark 1:15

He went on to point out that life sometimes gives us situations where we must choose an action, but like the man who slipped on a banana peel in the street just as the bus came around the corner, there is no time to make life's situations into 'problems'.

▶ To Be Here Now:

- Taste your next meal
- Smell your next flowers
- Sing and laugh in your next shower
- Look your loved one in the eye

- Let your next breath be deep and 'in-spire' you
- Hear the next birdsong outside your window
- Enjoy the scenery on your next drive
- Feel the pillow under your cheek as you lay yourself down to rest

▶ HOW TO BE THOUGHTLESS

Thoughtlessness is more loving and joyful than it might sound at first. It is thought that keeps us in analysis paralysis rather than in our simple, natural and joyful essence of being. For most people, the easiest analogy is the sexual experience. The more you 'think' about sex while involved in it, the less rich the experience. It is only when we surrender to the moment, to our sense of the natural flow, that our highest highs occur.

Similarly, the greatest athletes have a natural flow, a relaxation into 'the zone' that is famous for rendering performances far beyond any they could have 'thought up'. In these cases, where artistry and grace take over the brain's attempts to 'do it right', there are no limits to our success.

Spiritual oneness with all that is, like sexual oneness with our partner, or 'being the ball', is not something that makes you think, it's something that ultimately allows you to stop thinking. All beingness is not only exhilarating, it is fun. We lose track of time; we get caught up.

Tolle, author of *The Power of Now*, points out that this is the attraction of death-defying feats such as mountain climbing or racecar driving. They are thrilling because the brain is so consumed in the moment that no worries or regrets can enter. We can achieve this thrill without backpacks or crash helmets, but we will have to overcome our fears just the same.

Remember the "Been there. Done that" slogan of the late '90's? It was a wake-up call telling us that we had fallen asleep to the magnificence of the moment. To help me remember that Now holds everything I could ever want if only I will allow myself to see it and be grateful for it, I have created a new refrigerator magnet:

Never Been Here. Never Done This.

Perhaps the most freeing of all the 12 habits, Be Here Now takes no time, no moving to a different place or achieving a new level of anything. It is the golden gem of this moment, shining within us, that we can 'mine' instantly.

When I was young, my mother used to say "Now, Now." I believe she, from her enlightened state, was calling me back to this moment from the terrors of tomorrow and the disappointments of days gone by. It was great advice.

There's no need to look further for what we seek. Every day can be our happy re-birthday, for this present is always open.

...I once was lost, but Now I'm found,
was blind, but Now I see.

From the gospel hymn, *Amazing Grace*

Change Your Thoughts ⓒ

The greatest discovery of my generation is that human beings,
by changing the inner attitudes of their minds,
can transform the outer aspects of their lives.

William James

▶ HOW TO LIVE HAPPILY EVER AFTER

Using a percentage between 0 and 100, how important do you think Attitude is for:

- health? _____

- wealth? _____

- success? _____

- happiness? _____

It is no secret that the happiest, healthiest and wealthiest among us tend to have more positive attitudes. When I ask 2000 nurses how important attitude is to the recovery process, they tell me 90–100%. When I ask the CEO's of multi-million dollar corporations how important attitude is to wealth, they tell me 90–100% as well. Whenever I ask professional athletes how important attitude is to success in competition, they always say 110%!

Every group I survey, from housewives to the homeless, agree that attitude is *The Most Important Factor* in getting what we want. Yet, when I ask them to define this incredibly powerful component, there is no consensus whatsoever!

NOTE: *This author does not believe that you can live or teach a positive attitude until you clearly understand what it is!*

I put the following words to music for a group of jr. high students years ago:

You hold the key to unlock any door
You hold the key you've been looking for...

"What is the key?" I asked them. There was great dissension among them.

Change Your Thoughts

So, what is attitude? The thesaurus on my computer brings up more than a dozen synonyms, such as "a way of behaving," "thoughts" and "feelings." Take a moment to answer this question for yourself:

Is **attitude** primarily a set of feelings, behaviors or beliefs?

(No, you cannot choose all three!)

_____

Yes, it's true that all three of the above components are affected by attitude. But for the ultimate source of attitude, we'll go to the ultimate source of universal truths:

Attitude: a state of mind.

Webster's Dictionary

▶ Not Feelings?

If positive attitude were simply a set of feelings, then, since there are neutral feelings, i.e. "I feel neutral about that," there would be neutral attitudes, which there are not. You'll never hear anyone's attitude described as 'neutral'!

If positive attitude were just a set of feelings, then you could not feel mad or sad and still have a positive attitude. But it is possible to feel mad or sad and have a very positive (FGH) attitude, or high Score, at the same time. We simply can use those feelings as a catalyst or trampoline to bounce us back into a positive frame of mind.

As it turns out, an individual with positive attitude will experience all of his or her feelings without judging them. Some, like anger, tend to be shorter-lived, but to hide from any one feeling will cause attitude problems. Those who have a flexible rather than a rigid range of emotions have more positive attitudes. Those who can get upset about what they don't want are much more likely to go for what they do! Therefore, attitude is not a set of 'good' and 'bad' feelings, although we 'feel better' when we are in a positive frame of mind. (More about feelings in the chapter on Habit F.)

▶ Not behaviors?

Likewise, attitude is not a set of behaviors, for negative attitudes can lurk just beneath both a pasted-on smile or a nice deed for the neighbors. Behaviors can sometimes sway your beliefs (i.e. volunteering at a homeless shelter) and sometimes cause a temporary shift in your feelings, but it is not your behaviors that will ultimately change your life. To believe in change only through behaviors would be like believing that hard work will make you rich. My friends and I decided long ago that if hard work alone was what made a person wealthy, we would all have been millionaires at 30!

Change Your Thoughts

▶ Yes, Beliefs!

Positive attitude is, first and foremost, *a set of thoughts and beliefs.* These beliefs are not a personality predisposition or inherent in our genes, but rather sit deep within us as universal truths with which we can reconnect one thought at a time. We can choose to repent, or re-think, teachings we have carried within us since childhood, unlearning so that we can relearn what is true for us in the present.

Be transformed by the renewing of your mind.

Romans 12:2

It is our thoughts and the resulting emotions, not our behaviors, which determine our inner Score and attract positive or negative to us. It is not the case that if we just behave in a decent way we will get good things in return, despite our negative thoughts or intentions. This is one of the greatest misunderstandings of the average self-improvement program.

When we dwell upon the negative aspects of life, thinking about what awful things could happen, what someone did to us, how we don't deserve good things because we messed up, etc., we get into a negative feeling place/Score and attract more of the same. We get what we think about throughout the day.

Where thought goes, energy flows.

▶ THE LAW OF ATTRACTION

The law of attraction is one of the universal laws that explains how things work. Things/thoughts that are alike, that have similar Scores, are drawn to each other. It's as simple as that.

It is as though you are a magnet. Let's say that one day you say to a friend, "I had some staples fly up and hit me in the face yesterday. It was really weird." No harm done in describing this incident, is there? You were just telling the truth. You didn't call anybody names. You didn't take out a lawsuit against the staples company. No big deal, right?

Wrong. For those of us who want greater happiness, our thoughts *are* a big deal, *actually,* the only deal in town. The law of attraction by our thoughts is always at work. When the ancient scriptures remind us that if we ask we shall receive, they do not add a footnote: "but you'll receive only the *good* things you think about." *Everything* we think about and talk about and have strong feelings about will come boomeranging back to be our blessing or bother.

As a man thinks, so he is. Proverbs 23:7

So, back to our story: After thinking and speaking about the staples for the next few days, one day you discover you have a new story to tell...

"You won't believe *this*! Today these *nails* came out of nowhere and hit me in the head!" Now you have every excuse to tell this dramatic story. You were a 'helpless victim' according to your perception. And everyone gathers around to hear the awful details.

The following day, what do you know, you have an even more amazing story. "A crowbar came out of **nowhere**!" And the story continues until one day *an anvil* gets your attention and you think to yourself, "Something's not right here..."

What's not 'right', or at least not helpful in this situation, are your thoughts and beliefs.

THE FGH FORMULA

So what is the difference between a positive attitude belief and a negative one? As we discussed in the chapter on Habit B, positive beliefs center around F, G or H. All thoughts that move us toward a positive attitude comprise either Forgiveness of the past, Gratitude for the present, or Hope for the future.

Our core beliefs are either positive (FGH) or negative (unforgiving, ungrateful and hopeless). As I said above, you've never heard anyone's attitude described as 'neutral'. If you're not in FGH, you're in a negative attitude mindset. Period.

A belief is simply a thought you *keep* thinking *until you feel it*. If you are feeling unattractive, you cannot attract beauty. When you feel unhealthy, you cannot attract health. Your mental/emotional state, your attitude, is the basis from which you attract life to you. When you see yourself as you want to be, and focus on those thoughts until you start to feel the accompanying feelings, then and only then will all good things come to you.

> *Whatever you pray for, believe you have it already,*
> *and it shall be yours.*
>
> Matthew 21:22

▶ THE FAX ABOUT ATTITUDE

The first time I saw a photo come out of a fax machine hooked to a phone line, I was shocked. How was this possible? The memory of that event reminds me of how I felt the day I 'got' that our thoughts had creative and attractive powers. Thoughts, like the impulses running through the telephone line to the fax, are simply energy moving from one point to another, creating the pictures we see as 'reality'.

OUR BRAIN-COMPUTER

If you bought a new computer game today and loaded it into your operating system, the first question on the screen might be "What is your name?" If you typed in your name as "Godzilla," would the computer *believe* you? Absolutely! And so does your brain.

Our brain is a kind of mega-computer that never shuts off. An offhand remark to a friend, such as "I am bad with numbers. I always get those two phone numbers mixed up," becomes a command/enter to our brain-computer.

> *It's about thinking on purpose, pondering on purpose,*
> *remembering on purpose, observing on purpose.*
>
> Abraham-Hicks

Change Your Thoughts ⓒ

It is crucial that we program our brain-computers for success and happiness. The good news is that programming the brain is simple; no expertise is needed. If we repeat over and over what we want to believe, and start to imagine it, pretend it, visualize it, eventually we will have a 'shift' where belief happens. We don't even need to believe what we are saying at first, as we'll see later.

We start transforming our thoughts by listening to them and 'catching them'. This can be easier said than done, as we have hundreds every minute. But starting with one thought at a time, the transformation takes on speed and momentum, often with startling results. Here is my promise:

▶ **Change your thoughts for 21 seconds a day for 21 days and you will become a Magnet for Miracles.**

Change thoughts to what? Gratitude. As we'll discuss in the next chapter, it is possible to find something to be grateful for in every moment, every person, every circumstance (even if it's gratitude that we are becoming clearer on what we *don't* want and know we have the power to attract better!).

How can such a thing be? Because, like the modem through a fax line, your thoughts send out signals. Ever 'felt' someone was looking at you from across the room, only to discover that they were? How can you explain that, except that there was something 'sent' to you from that person?

We are constantly sending signals out from us, and these 'signals' are thoughts at a certain vibrational level or Score. What happens as we flow through life is that we attract people and experiences at the Score of our thoughts. The higher the Scores, the more we are allowing the flow of all that is good, peaceful, easy and joyful.

To make this point more clearly, let's assign numbers to our thoughts.

Who has more energy, a positive attitude (FGH) person or a negative attitude person? Of course, the former. Therefore, we'll give thoughts of F, G or H, as discussed in the last chapter, a positive (+) number.

If the majority of your thoughts are FGH, your present Score might equal +78. If, on the other hand, your thoughts are full of worry, anxiety, blame or regret, your Score might be –28.

Now let's imagine a –28 and a +78 going out for lunch together. Can you see how one might feel drained after the event? The –28 isn't a bad person, just a needy one. They have created such a negative space through their thinking that their goal during the meal is less to be nourished with food than to get nourished with energy — energy they must get from somewhere.

In physics, you will never hear that when cold energy is joined with hot energy, that the cold loses its (cold) energy to the heat but rather that the heat loses its (heat) energy to the cold. Same concept.

Some people brighten up the whole room by leaving it.

Zig Ziglar

Change Your Thoughts Ⓒ

Does this mean we should never offer our warmth to someone who, to us, is cold? Certainly not. But if our goal is to change them, that judgment will lower *our* temperature. Our goal must simply be gratitude and love.

More on how we protect against having our energy drained will be covered in the chapter on Habit I. For now, let's just reaffirm which of these two people at lunch we are determined to be!

So how do you achieve the 21-day Miracle Magnetism? Each day morning and/or evening, stop for 21 seconds and think or speak a stream of gratitude phrases. All sorts of recent things you're grateful for. They don't need to be related.

To speed up the process even more, whenever you catch yourself 'out of the flow' of FGH in worry, fear, regret, or ingratitude, move back into a *gratitude thought.*

Oftentimes I will change my thought to something completely different by reading a positive magazine article, petting my dog, turning on my favorite music, etc. The really exciting truth is that simply by getting into gratitude and the good feelings it brings, we can raise our Score immediately. By changing a thought here or there, we become a positive magnet, and soon raise our Score to attract the life of our dreams with ease.

For example, one woman I know was extremely critical of men and could often be heard blaming the entire gender for the problems of the world. One day she was especially upset about men "sizing up women's bodies." After she calmed down, I asked her if she liked her body. She admitted she did not. When we discussed what she could do to start thinking and feeling differently about her appearance, her attitude moved toward FGH and her negativity lifted. She had raised her Score in just minutes.

> *The happiness of your life*
> *depends upon the quality of your thoughts.*
>
> Marcus Aurelius

This material can be jolting if you have never been exposed to it before. Take a deep breath and reflect upon how you might integrate this into your own belief system with the following questions:

If it were true that all I needed to do was think more gratitude thoughts to attract daily miracles into my life...

_____

_____

_____

_____

_____

If it were true that every time my thoughts and words dwell on what I don't want, I am attracting those very things into my life...

_____

_____

_____

_____

_____

▶ TOUCHSTONES

One of the ways I use this 'key' of changing my thoughts in every day life is to go to a touchstone. A touchstone is a small symbol of a big wonderful memory or a big dream. I once asked each of 40 men in a shelter for the one of their memories that brought them the most joy.

I heard of the one time in his 62 years of life that a father told his son that he loved him... I heard of a man holding his son and namesake in his hands for the first time... I heard of a grandfather taking his grandson aside and telling him that of all the grandchildren, he would be the one to be taught the grandfather's trade... Each one had a touching story of a powerful moment in time, a moment that can be recaptured whenever there is need for a positive thought.

The other kind of touchstone that can transform us is a dream. In the next chapter we'll talk about creating a physical picture of your dreams, but for now, any photo, movie or mental image will do. Choose one that is a sure-fire feel good and then come back to it again and again. Make it a familiar friend.

The brain cannot distinguish between a thought and reality.

Sometimes it's good to have more than one touchstone. For example, you could have one for work and one for your personal life. Find something in nature that is a physical representation of each touchstone and put it in a special place where you can see it each day.

What are some of my touchstones?

_____

_____

_____

Change Your Thoughts

 ### The Power of Placebos

If the power of our thoughts and beliefs is so great, why do we not use them to feel better physically as well as emotionally? Many people do.

We can choose to say something 'makes us sick', or we can choose to catch such phrases as they come out of our mouths. What actually is 'making us sick' is not the external event, but our thought response to it. Turning our thoughts and words to, "I felt great when I heard..." moves us closer to the health we long for.

One example of this is the power of the placebo effect. In a 1999 study done by Harvard University, its effectiveness was tested in a wide range of disturbances. In a trial to test the value of the surgical procedure to treat angina pectoris, (chest pain,) the placebo procedure consisted in anesthetizing the patient and only cutting his skin. The patients thus fictitiously treated showed an 80% improvement while of those actually operated upon, the improvement was only 40%. In other words: placebo acted better than surgery.

Why are placebos so effective? Because we believe they are.

Our subconscious can't take a joke.
Dr. Bobbie Summers, Ph.D.

From Thought to Feeling

Thoughts generate primarily by transforming our feelings. Notice how you *felt* after doing the last writing exercise about your touchstones. It is amazing how quickly our thoughts take a feeling effect. Thoughts even slow down our pulse or warm our hands. Once we feel differently, we act differently, which eventually transforms our lives. I remember it this way because it's in reverse alphabetical order:

What we <u>t</u>hink

 determines what we <u>f</u>eel,

determines what we <u>d</u>o and <u>g</u>et,

determines who we <u>a</u>re.

Now, add to this the fact that research has shown that the brain cannot distinguish between an actual experience and an imagined one. It is easy to see why we cannot afford the high price of a negative thought.

The Me in the Media

I have long been an advocate of media-free living. I encourage people to take regular (and long) breaks from 'the news', as this generation calls body-bag journalism. And yet I have often been as negative as any of the newspapers or nightly newscasts I was condemning.

I can begin my Monday morning by rehashing things that went awry over the weekend. I can fill my walking time with an hour of what is wrong with the world. I can waste hours on end stewing about something I should have said to my friend.

The goal is to 'turn the channel' when my mind gets into negative thoughts. Remember, 'negative' is anything not in harmony with FGH; being negative means being unforgiving, ungrateful and hopeless.

> *Whatever you put your attention on will grow stronger in your life.*
> *Whatever you take your attention away from will wither,*
> *disintegrate and disappear.*
>
> Dr. Deepak Chopra

At this point in my seminars, I am often asked, "But how can I monitor my thoughts? They come too fast..." The good news is that just catching one per day will change your life dramatically for the better.

A tall 40-something gentleman came to a class I was offering recently with drooped shoulders. "I just don't seem to have any energy," he began. "There are so many things I should be doing, but I find I get trapped into worrying how things will turn out, where the money will come from, dozens of things..."

I asked him to simply keep track of one worry thought each day. I encouraged him to write it down and then record the time when it occurred. Just one per day. To his and the group's amazement, he stood taller and talked more energetically every week. By the time of our graduation he was building an addition onto his home, a project he'd put off for years.

I invite circumstances and people into my life through my thoughts, which turn into emotions. We become what we think about and talk about all day.

It's 10 o'clock. Do you know where your thoughts are?

▶ **THE POWER OF SELF-TALK**

One simple way to monitor how our thoughts are going is by listening to our self-talk. In order to redirect your thoughts, learn to replace 'helpless' phrases with 'hero' phrases:

Helpless Talk		Hero Talk
"I should..."	*becomes*	"I want..."
"I can't..."	*becomes*	"I haven't yet..."
"He/She makes me..."	*becomes*	"I feel _____ when..."
"That was stupid..."	*becomes*	"That was interesting..."
"I'll try..."	*becomes*	"I'll do my best..."
"I am upset/tired..."	*becomes*	"I feel a little upset/tired..."

Also: When we get into thoughts of 'never' and 'always', we are in destructive criticism of ourselves or others. We can rephrase those thoughts by describing what is happening for us *right now*.

C ▶ **LOSING THE WAIT**

I learned about the power of self-talk early in my recovery period. When I first started offering classes in my home, a woman shared, "The holidays are coming, and since I'm going to visit my family, I really *should* lose this weight..."

At this point, the woman next to her interrupted excitedly. She held up the self-talk list above and asked, "Would you like to rephrase that?"

After looking at the sheet, the first woman replied, "Oh no! I don't *want* to lose the weight!" We were all amazed. After a moment of stunned silence, I asked her what she *did* want to do.

"Well, I'd love to travel."

"So why don't you travel?" I asked.

"Oh, I've got to lose the weight first."

It was obvious to us that she could lose the weight, and lose the waiting, when she was ready. As it was, she was sending her brain a very clear imperative, "I don't want to lose the weight." When we use such a phrase, the brain replies with a simple, "No problem." Then it goes about its task of slowing the metabolism or changing our cravings, so that even if we do attempt to diet, we won't find long-term success.

▶ **I SHOULDN'T SHOULD ON MYSELF**

Once when I was teaching my program to a military base, a gentleman threw out the following challenge to the group: "I *should* mow my lawn before inspection tomorrow morning, but I don't want to. How will I explain my newfound freedom to my commanding officer?"

I asked him if he *wanted* to live on base. When he answered, "Yes," I reminded him that whenever we make a choice, responsibilities accompany it. He knew the rules when he signed on for base housing. He now had a commitment to keep until he made other arrangements. He agreed to change his self-talk to, "I want to mow my lawn, because I want to live on base."

Once we understand the power of self-talk, we become more aware of the amazing things we have been telling our brains. Recently, I noticed I was sending a negative message whenever my children argued. "I am tired of you two fighting!" I would say, and sure enough, I'd need a nap before the day was over. As soon as I started saying, " I want you two to cooperate, or I will separate you," they weren't arguing so much and I wasn't so tired.

> *Nothing is more important than thinking thoughts*
> *that make you feel good.*
>
>   Abraham-Hicks

Get back to a thought that feels good. One of my favorite things to do in my home or office is amazingly simple, but it works for me. I excuse myself to go to the bathroom and wash my hands with a very fragrant soap. I splurge on nice soaps (or bring them back from

Change Your Thoughts

the nicest motels!). I allow myself to take my time and inhale the fragrance during the process. I come out 'clean' of the old thoughts every time, even if only temporarily. Temporarily is fine, because that's all we have to deal with, this moment.

▶ THE MEANING IN THE MESSAGE

Many people want to discard this formula of feeding our brain more positive messages as too simplistic. During one corporate seminar, I had a participant challenge me with, "This self-talk stuff... I just don't buy it!"

"Do you buy Pepsi?" I asked.

"Of course. What's that got to do with it?" he answered.

I then asked him what three-word national billboard campaign Pepsi was running at the time. "Gotta Have It," he replied.

"Is there any new product information in that slogan about price? Taste? Environmental safety?"

He shook his head. Then I asked him how it was that this campaign was one of the most successful ever used by the billion-dollar corporation. Could it be that we are simply giving our computer-brains the message: "(I) gotta have it?" every time we read the billboard?

If you're getting thirsty as you read this, don't be surprised. When Pepsi-Cola's marketing research says the billboard slogan works, chances are it does. Whether with billboards or self-talk, whatever your brain perceives, it believes.

▶ KEEPING SCORE WITH SELF-TALK

An example of the power of self-talk came from Julie, a high school junior who was taking my course. An avid golfer, Julie desperately wanted to earn a golf scholarship to college. "But I have to shoot an 85, and the lowest I've ever shot is a 92!" she lamented. "Will changing my self-talk help my golf score?"

We decided it couldn't hurt.

I asked Julie to walk around our circle of chairs, look each of us in the eye and say, "I'm shooting an 85 this summer." At first she resisted, but by the end of the circle we could hear a new determination in her voice. We applauded her for having the courage to say her dream out loud.

Later that week while out golfing with her father, Julie shot her first 85. A fluke? Perhaps. But if you argue with Julie, she'll ask you to explain how she won a tournament just two weeks later with an 80. She'll also ask you to explain why just about every pro golfer has a sports psychologist on their staff.

Julie got her golf scholarship and called to thank me. She added that there was one negative upshot, however.

"What's that?" I asked.

"Now my top competitor has caught onto self-talk!" she giggled.

We both knew that with life's wonderful abundance, Julie's mind-set was the only real hindrance, and she had now learned to get out of her own way.

After experiencing events like these, I don't have to give teens lectures on why the hopeless lyrics of many of today's songs are not in their best interest. They learn from life experience that what you put into your mind will come out in your life.

Thoughts held in mind, produce after their kind.

Unity saying

► USING AFFIRMATIONS

To help achieve our dreams and goals, it's not only important to avoid negative self-talk, but to replace it with positive affirmations. Since our computer brain is so responsive to whatever we tell it, why not program it for the very best? Affirmations are simply positive programming.

The most effective affirmations have four characteristics in common. They are:

- Personal (I)
- Present Tense (am)
- Pleasurable (enjoying)
- Positive (new characteristic)

When I add 'positive' to the list, I am often asked how an affirmation could be anything but positive. I explain that the brain works on pictures and has no picture for the word 'not'.

► DON'T SAY DON'T ☺

This sub-heading makes a silly but important point. When we ask our mind or the minds of others *not* to do something, it usually backfires. "Don't go in the street," spoken to a child, is a very powerful command to do just that. Her young but very powerful brain is a computer screen for pictures. She gets the picture 'street' and focuses upon it. It literally draws her into danger. A simple rephrasing such as, "Stay on this grass now," will do more to accomplish a concerned parent's goal.

I recall speaking to a "Keep America Beautiful" group and discussing this concept of focusing on what we want, rather than on what we do not want. The story that came from a participant made us all smile:

"It was our annual clean-up day for our small community and we were putting together the fliers for the event when two different groups in town contacted us, asking that there be no dogs allowed at the event. We decide to add to the flier, 'Please do not bring your dogs'. As a result, the dog problem was so bad this year that we're still dealing with the upsets and messes months later."

Here are some more everyday examples of Nots that can get us all knotted up.

"I will not smoke anymore"	*becomes*	"I am really enjoying my clean, clear lungs"
"Don't forget to get the milk"	*becomes*	"Remember to bring home some milk"
"You can't trust those people"	*becomes*	"I am so appreciative of all the trustworthy people in my life."
"Just say No to Drugs"	*becomes*	"Just say Yes to feeling your feelings and living life to the full!"
"No shoplifting"	*becomes*	"Thanks for paying for the items you are taking with you."

It is important to be as specific as you can. When you are setting a goal with an affirmation, phrases such as, "I am enjoying the energy that comes from weighing 135 pounds," and "I am enjoying the freedom that comes from making $50,000 a year," accord with all of the guidelines.

The tale is true as long as the telling lasts...

▶ PLANNING YOUR PERSONAL PROGRAM

I used to do my best to 'do my affirmations' once or twice a day. Now that I understand the power of my thoughts, I make it my TOP priority to think thoughts that attract joy, health and prosperity *every moment.* My children, friends, co-workers and Mom are all aware of my priority. I have a group of folks that meet at my home once a week to remind and congratulate ourselves for our focus on positive, grateful thoughts.

Am I willing to make focusing and redirecting my thoughts a priority?

_____

How will I track progress of my miracle magnetizing? e.g., Check in with my coach or teammates regularly? Journal?

_____

_____

_____

_____

_____

_____

Change Your Thoughts Ⓒ

Many pleasures in life can bring us greater happiness. Many skills can be used to improve our attitude. None is more effective than changing what we focus upon.

> *All that we are arises with our thoughts.*
> *With our thoughts we make the world.*
>
> Buddha

Dream and Imagine

Go confidently in the direction of your dreams. Live the life you imagined.

Henry David Thoreau

Years after the filming of the movie *Field of Dreams*, a line of cars still winds down the road in Dyersville, Iowa, to visit a little baseball field in the middle of a corn field. It was estimated that over 50,000 tourists visited this site last year, making it the most popular tourist attraction in the state.

Don Lansing, the owner of the farm used as a setting for the film, does not charge for the visits. "You don't see any litter. Never one pop can. If somebody drops something, seven people reach to pick it up."

As a local reporter wrote, "Whatever they all come searching for, they inevitably find. That much is clear from their expressions as they leave."

What is the magic of a place like this? Why are our dreams so sacred? What is the power they carry? Are dreams an escape from reality or the very essence of reality? And why do we talk so much about dreams for young people, yet lose touch with dreams as we age? Do dreams *really* come true?

▶ Where Dreams Begin

To begin to answer these important queries, let's being with children's literature, rife with dreamy subjects. The story of Pinnochio, for example, reminds us of the importance of dreams. Like Gepetto, the puppeteer, we are encouraged to first carve out our dream, and to begin to believe in it. The next step is to either put it aside on a shelf and go about our business, or rest and relax. At some point later, it will be time to say our belief aloud — even if only to the kitten on our windowsill. Finally, we must follow our dream no matter what happens — even if it lands us on the bottom of the ocean in the belly of a whale.

For a modern day look at the power of dreams at work, one of my favorite examples is the 1993 movie *Rudy*, based on the true story of a young man who yearned to play football for the University of Notre Dame. His desire was so intense that he overcame bad grades, small stature, lack of exceptional talent, lack of money, and lack of support from family members. Yet, because of the tenacity with which he followed his dream, Rudy accomplished a feat no Notre Dame player has matched before or since.

When you dream, you don't read from the right side of the menu.

Refrigerator magnet

And then there are dreamers like Edison and Ghandi, Eleanor Roosevelt and Mother Teresa, Abe Lincoln and Martin Luther King, who each held to their dreams despite ridicule, moving nations and worlds as a result.

Dream and Imagine D

As a motivational and inspirational speaker, I train people in many components of a happy life. None seems to touch them like the encouragement and process of dreaming. Whenever we talk of being inspired by someone, we are usually referring to being touched by his or her dream of a better world. In order to find greater happiness, in order to manifest the miraculous, we must all stay in touch with our dreams.

Those who lose dreaming are lost.

Aborigine Proverb

Some time ago, I realized I had never met a kid on drugs who still had a dream. When speaking with a prominent juvenile court judge in our state, I asked him what he had found amidst all the tragedies he dealt with that gave him the greatest hope. The first thought that came to his mind was a program where fourth-graders were taken to college campuses for a day. "It gives them a dream," he said. "What they often lose early in life is hope."

Dreams are an energy source, not just for children, but for adults as well. My dreams motivate me to get up each morning and give my all. As the dream of this book draws closer to reality, already my next dreams are forming. Without a dream, we are simply going through the motions of life. Dreams are life giving and when we open ourselves to them, they can be counted on to transform our inner and outer worlds.

▶ THE FIRST STEP

"Oh no, there are even steps to *dreaming*?" Well, don't worry. They can't be too complicated or kids wouldn't be so darn good at it. In fact, for any children reading this book, you guys can skip this part. But, for the adults, yes, there are steps, ones that you and I have always known deep inside, but have forgotten. Allow me to gently remind us here, using our friend Gepetto's favorite dream:

The Pinnochio Formula:

1. Carve Out Your Dream
2. Believe in it
3. Release it or Speak it
4. Never give up

▶ Step 1: Carve Out Your Dream

The step that causes consternation in so many adults is to the child like their next breath of air: Get in touch with your desires.

In the chapter on Habit A we looked at how to ask people for things and how that takes a lot of courage. Well, getting in touch with our dreams takes 100 times more daring, for they are a deeper part of us that many of us have buried under years of efficiency and propriety so that they cannot hurt us.

How can dreams hurt? When we do not remember the formula for making dreams come true, it can feel like we were hoodwinked, betrayed, and abandoned by this very spiritual

Dream and Imagine

essence of our own being. In anger and hurt, then, not understanding our part in the process, we scoff at dreams and dreamers and try to cut off this part of ourselves. But dreams can never be cut off or buried for ever. They continue to live just beneath the surface, knowing that when the time is right, we will unearth them and once again breathe the life they carry.

Nothing is too good to be true,
Nothing is too wonderful to happen,
Nothing is too good to last.

When you dream, you imagine the overall effect. You can release the who, when, where and how. You just trust. Take the risk. Do this journaling. Even if you haven't done one other written exercise so far, write now.

Write down 5 or 6 of your dreams. A dream, remember, rather than a goal, is boundless, so dream in abundance. Imagine that you have unlimited time, resources, support, energy, health, and motivation. Imagine your home, your friends, your waistline, your garden, your neighbors, your bank account, your hobbies, your spirituality, your family, your freedom, your state of mind. What would you do if you could do anything at all? That's your dream. Write it on the blank lines on the following page.

If you're still not sure what your dreams are, I suggest the 'Lottery Winner' game:

Congratulations! You just won the lottery! It's your first year as a lottery winner: whatever will you do? Write it all down on a clean sheet of paper. (Fill it!)

Wow! What a great first year you've had since winning the lottery. But you're kind of tired of what you did last year, so what will you do this year? Write it all down on a new sheet of paper. (Good job!)

Gee Whiz! I can tell by looking at you that you're really kind of tired now. All that go-go-go for the last two years... now all you want to do is come home, huh?

Go home and have a nice long rest. You deserve it. (Your butler awaits you.)

Well, you look all rested. Hey, when you woke up this morning, you realized there are some things you've always wanted to do with your life. What are they?

Dream and Imagine   **D**

Write your Dreams here:

_____

_____

_____

_____

_____

_____

_____

_____

_____

_____

_____

_____

_____

_____

_____

▶ **Step 2: Believe In It**

Jim Carrey, an actor known for his zany comedy films, realized the importance of believing in his dreams. In an interview with Barbara Walters, he shared that in 1987, during a three-month stretch without work, he had only enough money for supper or a tank of gas. He chose to buy the gas, and drove to one of the most prestigious neighborhoods in Beverly Hills in the middle of the night.

When he found what he considered the most beautiful home in the area, he got out and sat on the curb with one intent — that he would not leave until he believed that he lived there. After hours of imagining his life as owner of the mansion, he could feel the feelings of knowing that those were his cars in the driveway and that his kids were sleeping on just the other side of that bedroom window. At this point, he got out his checkbook and wrote out a check to himself for $10 million, "for services rendered." He then dated the check "1995" and put it in his billfold.

It was in February of 1995 that Carrey received a real check for $10 million dollars for a film entitled *The Mask* that he had just completed. When he buried the dream check with his father one month later, the actor explained, "His dream was realized through me."

Miracles happen to those who believe in them.

Bernard Berenson

How do you get to a 'believing place' with your dreams? Writing them down is a good start. Drawing them, making a poster or collage of them, anything visual that will spark a physical as well as spiritual reaction is helpful when you are not yet 'a believer'.

A study of Harvard alumni found that ten years after graduation:

- 83% of the graduates had no specific goals that they could name, either personally or professionally.
- 14% had specific goals but had never written them down.
- 3% had written goals.

In an income comparison, the third group with the written goals (3%) was making ten times as much income as the first group with no goals (83%).

Don't just THINK it, INK it.

OK, kids of all ages, we're getting out the glue sticks and scissors. If you are not yet a believer, or even if you are a believer but have not seen some of your dreams manifest as quickly as you'd like, a collage is a powerful way to call forth your vision. Focus on one of your dreams right now.

✂ How to Make a Collage

For this 1–2 hour project you'll need:

- 1 poster board per dream
- 2 glue sticks
- scissors
- a dark-colored magic marker
- lots of different kinds of magazines (ask your friends for theirs)
- a space where you will not be interrupted (by anyone other than a friend you may ask to join in the process!)

First, find the exact phrasing of this dream-come-true. Remember, a dream is never about 'not' doing something. One dreamscape poster I have in my home right now says, "I publish 10 of my songs in the year 2000 as part of my enjoying being a successful composer." The time frame is optional. The phrase that is right for you will bring up feelings of joy and excitement. You will be writing it somewhere on the poster, large enough to be read from 3–6 feet away.

Next, get to the feeling place of what your dream will feel like when it is accomplished. This will just take a few minutes. Note if colors or pictures come to mind. Then, start cutting out pictures and words that pop out at you from the magazines as you sit in this dreamy place. The best collages have twice as many pictures as words. Remember, you don't need to explain to anyone why you chose a picture. This collage is for *you*.

Dream and Imagine Ⓓ

Now, begin to lay out the pictures and words on the poster board. Decide by experimentation where you want things to be. Feel free with this: e.g., pictures can overlap or be uneven. Make sure to include where your dreamphrase will be written. Once you've found a placement you're comfortable with, start writing and gluing!

Congratulations! Fun, wasn't it? Now place the dreamscape some place where you'll see it every day. If you have a walk-in closet or workspace you go to regularly, they work well, but feel free to mount it anywhere in your home!

You can't rely on your eyes when your imagination is out of focus.

Mark Twain

What did I experience as I created my collage?

_____

_____

_____

_____

_____

_____

_____

_____

Imagination sets the goal 'picture'
which our automatic mechanism works on.
We act, or fail to act, not because of 'will'
as is so commonly believed,
but because of imagination.

Maxell Maltz

▶ DAILY VISUALIZATION

In any endeavor the most successful people are those who practice the thoughts and feelings of success even before the success occurs. For this, one of the most powerful techniques is visualization. Everyone who can think of what his or her home looks like without having to be standing in front of it can visualize. It's simply seeing with the mind's eye.

In her book, *The Joy of Visualization*, Valerie Wells says, "A picture is worth a thousand words, and visualizing is worth a thousand efforts." As far back as the first century B.C., Virgil said, "Mind moves matter." With this reality in mind, don't save visualization just for the big dreams in your life. At our house we use it to forecast everything from a fun trip to the grocery store to an enjoyable garage-cleaning day!

Visualization is a good friend of mind.

Arnold Schwarzenegger commissioned an artist to make drawings of his body at a better-defined level than had ever been achieved by a body-builder. He knew he could achieve what he could conceive. Those were the pictures, according to Schwarzenegger, that helped him surpass all previous accomplishments in definition and muscle mass. Why he won, in his own words? "Because I saw myself so clearly, being up there on the stage and winning."

The best news, perhaps, is that this powerful mind-sight tool is easy. It takes just four or five minutes of your day or week. When you're sitting down, simply take a couple of deep breaths and daydream about how things will be, look and feel when your next goals are accomplished. Imagine not only the pictures of success, but also the smells, tastes, and sounds as well. Visualize in 3-D! The clearer the image, the easier it will be for your incredible brain-computer to 'get with the program'.

▶ Step 3: Release or Remind

Have you ever noticed that some of the things that you contemplate for only a few seconds then show up with absolutely no effort on your part? I have had many a friend tell me that they, like me, will think of someone or something they have not thought of for a while, and the phone will then ring or the item will appear. This is completely understandable once we grasp how dreaming works.

A dream is a very high Score item. When we are dreaming, we are at our peak. Once the thought occurs, the dream begins to come our way. However, we can begin to put up obstacles on its path (i.e., lower the Score) when we start to get into Non-FGH thoughts such as doubt, worry or judgment.

The good news is that when we, like Gepetto, change our thoughts to another topic, there is no time for these negative thoughts to 'clog up' the pathways that are bringing our dreams into reality. This leaves us with two options, both of which work beautifully: Release the dream once you've conceived it, or, if you cannot help but think about it, simply remind yourself that all is well and that it is coming your way as fast as it can.

Are you beginning to see where children have the advantage in the dream department? It is quite natural for them to conceive and believe in their dreams. They understand that that is how things work. Equally effortless is their ability to "Let Go and Let God," even with their most fervent prayers.

Last Christmas, the kids and I sent out the same Christmas present to everyone. Each individual or family on our list got *God Bags* (available through www.GodBag.com). I was truly impressed with the simple wisdom of these beautifully decorated paper bags whose instructions went as follows:

Dream and Imagine   **D**

1. Create a problem/challenge/dream (if you already have one, you can skip step one.)
2. Write it out and date it.
3. Open bag.
4. Insert problem/challenge/dream.
5. Close bag.
6. Let Go and Let God! (If you insist on thinking about the problem/challenge, or worse yet, meddling in it once it has been placed in the bag, remove the challenge and tell God, out loud, that you feel you can do a better job of it than He can.)

There is more, but you get the point! Life does not have to be a struggle. Dreams can be (and are) fulfilled with great ease when we least expect them.

> *These days, instead of pushing the river,*
> *I've decided to go with the flow.*
>
> Cheyenne Autumn

I remember one seminar when a gentleman in his 50's told us he had always wanted to drive a train. He said that he was embarrassed to bring up this childhood dream at such a 'ripe' age, but couldn't think of any other dreams to share with the group. I had started doing some training with Union Pacific that same week and knew the simulator was due in town the following week. He got to 'drive his train' after all!

▶ Step 4: Never Give Up

Every so often we'll hear, "Dreamers have their heads in the clouds!" This is true. We must rise above the crowd, above the status quo, to dream. The key to success is to also keep our feet on the ground, not giving up until we find fulfillment. We will discuss this further in the chapter on habit K, but one personal story is worth sharing here.

I woke up one morning with a thought of making a TV commercial thanking my adopted daughter's birth mother, whom I had never met. By mid-morning, the entire 30-second spot was clear to me: how she would be waving to her birthmom while I spoke, and then the camera would pan out to hundreds of parents saying thank you as they held their adopted, waving children. I began calling various media and community groups that I thought might help me. They all thought it was a good idea. None of them, however, volunteered any support. I decided it must have been a bad idea and dropped it.

> *There are no private thoughts.*
>
> *A Course in Miracles*, Lesson 19

Four years later, I got a call from one of the gentlemen I had contacted that day. He worked with a social services agency and said he had seen my commercial. Since at the time I appeared frequently on camera as a spokesperson, I asked which commercial he was referring to. "The one you called me about a few years back, the Mother's Day commercial. It's powerful, Mary Kay, and it's touching women like you wouldn't believe."

When I told him I had never followed through with the idea, he was truly amazed. What he had seen was someone else's effort that was exactly as I had described. While he affirmed me for my idea, I mourned that I had not had the persistence and courage to complete the project years before.

Hold fast to dreams, for if dreams die,
life is a broken-winged bird that cannot fly.

Langston Hughes

▶ DREAMING FOR OUR KIDS

A friend of mine had a dream for his inner-city grade school: that every child would have the opportunity to attend not only the finest high schools, but the finest colleges in the area.

Four years after he began to share his dream with others, he received funding from a prominent citizen in the community to offer both gifts to every graduating eighth-grader. Today, if the students stay out of trouble with the law, do not get pregnant, and achieve passing high school grades, their reward is a full four-year scholarship to one of seven colleges and universities in the area.

Educators and presidents have honored the grade school and its achievements dozens of times. But its greatest reward is the track record for success that these hope-full children have begun, including a 0% unemployment rate for graduates!

Look around you right now. Everything you see, including the furniture you're sitting on, began in someone's mind. So must our dreams.

▶ GETTING YOUR GOAL-CARD!

How is a dream different from a goal? They are vastly different. A dream cannot be too big, while a goal cannot be too small. As one woman was learning to set goals, she wrote, "I will be more patient." She had no mental picture of this goal, thus setting herself up for disappointment and self-rejection. As author Maria Nemeth notes in her book, *The Energy of Money,* it is better to make our goals SMART:

Specific
Measurable
Attainable
Relevant
Time-Based

As one successful CEO told me, "I'd rather under-promise and over-deliver." We can set new goals once we've surpassed our smaller ones, but the feeling of accomplishment will make that next level of goal all that much easier. We must feel good to attract good.

I asked the woman for a specific time when she was impatient and discovered she wanted to be more patient with her young children in the morning. She then changed her goal to, "I will lay out the kids' clothes the night before school three times this week." It was a small enough goal, met all of the SMART criteria, and in a very short time made her feel successful and in control. Those good feelings allowed her to start dreaming again, and raised her Score for happiness.

D

Dream and Imagine

▶ CAN WE RUN OUT OF DREAMS?

A young man from an inner-city high school once asked me if I wasn't feeling empty now that so many of my dreams had come true. I assured him that the joy I felt from having accomplished my past dreams only gave me more courage to dream bigger dreams. "But what if you run out of dreams?" he asked sincerely.

Then I asked him if there were still people hurting in the world. "Of course!" he said.

"As long as there are," I assured him. "I'll never run out of dreams. And neither will you." I wanted to give my friend hope, but I also had to remind him that it isn't always easy.

Our corporation, Insight Inc., has changed thousands of lives. But in the early months of our business, I remember a phone call from someone close to me. As I told him of my new venture, his response was, "Oh, everything you're into is such a fad!" I politely told him that my dream was too young and fragile to survive such harsh words, and I needed to end the phone call. When I was able to call him back a few months later, he apologized, recommended my tape series to a friend, and subscribed to our newsletter. (Note: our newsletter is now free of charge on the web at www.marykaymueller.com.)

Sometimes, when we first give life to our dreams, we must protect them from attack. But following our dreams is always worth the effort. When we follow them, not only do we find happiness, but as Gepetto discovered, everyone around us becomes more real.

▶ A YOUNG BOY'S DREAM

Not long ago I came across the following true story of a poor working class boy raised in a large English city. Music and art were not part of his regular environment but one day his school took him to a concert in the city's Town Hall. He went prepared to be bored but was electrified by artists who made music fun. He particularly remembered an impassioned performance of "The Flight of the Bumblebee." To his chagrin the experience was never repeated, and it became his dream to rectify that.

When he became Leader of the City Council years later, he got the central government to pass legislation to dedicate 60 acres of one of the city's public parks to be a Regional Arts Center. On wooded lawns beside a winding river they built three centers for the performing arts, studios for those practicing music, painting, singing, dance, and workshops for carpentry and other crafts. The principle was that a child or any young person could visit and try out his or her skills in any direction with expert help and supervision. If they found a medium they really enjoyed, they could take it further. The rule was that adults could do the same, if accompanied by a child.

It truly "makes no difference who you are." Your dreams can come true.

Everything you ask for and pray for,
believe that you have it already,
and it shall be yours.

Mark 11:24

Expect a Miracle (E)

The real act of discovery consists not in finding new lands,
But in seeing with new eyes.

Marcel Proust

"If you look the right way, you can see the whole world is a garden." After viewing the movie, *The Secret Garden*, this was the line that stayed with my 5-year-old. While the credits rolled, he turned to me and asked, "Mom, what's the right way?" I told him it was a wonderful and very important question.

How we perceive life affects how much we enjoy life. Individuals with positive attitudes are optimistic; they expect the best. Although not everyone is raised with this mind-set, it can be learned. And once we understand the extraordinary benefits of optimistic or hopeful thinking, we will want to do just that.

Optimism is a set of beliefs based on the following tenets:

1. The bad things in life are temporary (limited in time).
2. The bad things in life are small or insignificant (limited in scope).
3. I have control over my environment.

Pessimistic beliefs are based on the opposite tenets:

1. The good things in life are temporary.
2. The good things in life are small or insignificant.
3. I have little or no control. Rather, I am a victim of my environment.

Optimists and pessimists are both right about the same number of times.
Optimists just enjoy life more.

A co-worker once confronted one of my good friends with, "You aren't really happy. You just think you're happy!" To which my friend replied, "Yeah, you're probably right, but self-brainwashing is a wonderful way to live." How happy we are is all in our minds.

What are some of the advantages of thinking optimistically? Optimistic and hopeful thinking relaxes us. Relaxation results in increased blood flowing to the brain, which means increased creativity and increased energy. In his wonderful book, *Learned Optimism*, Martin Seligman, Ph.D., cites hundreds of studies demonstrating that optimists:

- are healthier
- give up less easily
- are more successful in school
- are more successful on the job
- are more successful on the playing field
- are more successful in relationships
- have children who are more successful in the above areas
- are depressed less often, and for shorter periods of time

In short, if we want to be happy, optimism is our thinking pattern of choice.

Expect a Miracle (E)

Making optimism a way of life can restore your faith in yourself.

Lucille Ball

In order to become more optimistic, we need to understand and assume the thoughts of an optimistic individual. First, let's look at the three beliefs of optimists and pessimists in greater detail.

▶ TEMPORARY VS. PERMANENT

First, a pessimist believes negative events are permanent. An optimist believes negative events are temporary. They see one adverse event, e.g., "I didn't get the job," as a temporary setback and may surmise, "No problem. I've heard it takes three to six months of looking to secure a really good position." The optimist knows that there are dozens of ways to achieve any particular goal.

From the same job rejection, the pessimist might conclude, "I'll never get a job." The pessimist sees one negative event as 'just the beginning' of bad things ahead and concludes, "I'm doomed."

Take the OPTIMISM QUIZ

This exercise will help you determine if you are presently optimistic or pessimistic. Take a moment to reflect on your life in recent months. Which have you interpreted as temporary flukes?

When things go well or poorly?

_____

People treating you well or harshly?

_____

Good government or corrupt government?

_____

Peace or discord?

_____

Health or illness?

_____

Success or failure?

_____

If you answered that the positive options above were the temporary components of life, you tend toward pessimism. Remember the good news — according to Seligman, pessimistic thinking can be reversed. "One of the most significant findings in psychology in the last twenty years is that individuals can choose the way they think." To think otherwise would, in itself, be pessimistic.

> *In the midst of winter, I finally learned that*
> *there was in me an invincible summer.*
>
> Albert Camus

► EXAGGERATION OF THE NEGATIVE

The second tendency of pessimists is to expand the areas affected by a negative event into 'everyone', or 'everything I do'. The times I have listened to individuals immersed in despair, they often greatly exaggerate the scope of the painful events in their lives. One negative encounter, such as rudeness from a salesperson, becomes "(all) people are so rude nowadays."

Take away their ability to exaggerate the negative, and we rob pessimists of their doom and gloom philosophy. Optimists, on the other hand, tend to restrict the negative influence to the specific occurrence or individual involved, while holding onto their personal power to take action and change it next time. The first time a salesperson is rude, an optimistic response might be, "He was probably just having a bad day," or "He is just reflecting my own negative expectations. I'm going to get into Gratitude thinking."

My children have poetry contests every year at their school. We usually write our own poems, but there are a few, like "It Couldn't Be Done" by Edgar Guest that are worth a child's hard work to get into his or her brain!

> *...There are thousands to tell you it cannot be done*
> *There are thousands to prophecy failure*
> *There are thousands to point out to you one by one*
> *the dangers that wait to assail you.*
>
> *But just buckle right in with a bit of a grin*
> *Just take off your coat and go to it*
> *Just start to sing as you tackle the thing*
> *That cannot be done and you'll do it!*
>
> Edgar Guest

► ACTION VS. BROODING

Finally, because of their belief in their own power, optimists tend to be action-oriented rather than ruminators, according to Seligman. Their rosier view of the world encourages action and their actions create a rosier world. Pessimists tend to live more in their heads.

Expect a Miracle (E)

They see other people and circumstances as having control over their lives and often fall into a "What's the use?" mentality. They feel helpless, which in turn makes them more hopeless.

"No Victims, only Volunteers" thinking and ownership of personal power create greater optimism.

> *Unfortunately, we have been taught to believe that*
> *negative equals realistic*
> *and positive equals unrealistic.*
>
> Susan Jeffers

▶ BETTER, NOT BITTER

Optimists not only believe that the negative is limited in time and scope, they often see it as blessing. They truly believe that good will come from pain. As an example, at a fairly early age Martin Seligman had the misfortune to watch his father's debilitating helplessness resulting from multiple strokes. Yet, it was only because of this painful circumstance that Seligman began his research into helplessness, giving hope to millions through his books and tapes on optimistic living.

> *These are not dark days; these are great days*
> *— the greatest days our country has ever lived.*
>
> Winston Churchill

Ask yourself these questions:

1. What is it I expect? Do I get it?

_____

_____

_____

_____

2. Who do I know who almost always choose to expect a miracle and then stay open to the possibilities?

_____

_____

_____

_____

3. How do I react to their optimism? With Envy? Mockery? Disbelief? Heightened motivation?

_____

_____

_____

_____

▶ THE OPTIMIST-PESSIMIST GAME

To improve our awareness of how negative or positive our mind-set is at any given time, we can practice optimism in the form of a game.

The following stories are real life experiences. With a friend, see who can think up the most exaggerated, worst possible negative outcome for each occurrence. Then, see who can visualize the most exaggerated, best possible positive outcome for each one. After you've finished, keep reading to find out what really happened.

▶ Example:

1. A 16 year-old's good friend fails to return her greeting as they pass in the hall between third and fourth period on a particular Monday morning.

    Worst possible outcome thoughts: I know she's mad that I talked to Mark at the party Saturday... She'll never speak to me again!... I am a really fickle friend... I can't even study for Spanish, I'm too upset... Why can't I keep good friends?

    Best possible outcome thoughts: She'll get over it... She'll understand when she finds out we were just talking about her... She's too good a friend to give up on us for one little thing... I can handle this... I'll talk to her after school and straighten things out...

Now it's your turn. Describe the worst and best possible outcomes for the following situations:

2. A young couple who has been trying to get pregnant for three years goes to a "Fertility of the Mind" seminar.

3. A banker is passed over for consideration for a promotion that she thinks she honestly deserved.

4. Missing her keys, a teacher asks in the faculty lounge if anyone has seen them. She is told, "Kevin Smith probably took them. I'm glad you've got him this semester instead of me!"

5. A gentleman goes to the wrong airport in Washington D.C. and isn't able to make it to the correct one in time to catch his flight.

6. A teller at a branch office of a financial institution cashes a thousand dollar check

for a customer, only to find that her computer was not updated in time to discover that the woman's account was closed.

7. A radio voice talent goes in for an audition, is told she is wonderful, and is then asked if she would be available the following Thursday. She tells the producer that Thursday would be great, but two Thursdays come and go without a call from the producer.

8. A 17-year-old doesn't find his name on the callback list for the musical, even though he had the lead in the musical the year before.

9. A corporate trainer is doing a class on assertiveness when a young woman jumps up and runs out of the room.

How did you do? Was it easier to think optimistically or pessimistically? Compare your optimistic responses with the real-life outcomes that follow...

1. The 16-year-old girl's friend saw her after school and started chatting about things as usual. When the confused girl asked why she hadn't responded to the earlier greeting, her friend said she didn't even hear her, probably because she was worried about the chemistry test that was next on her schedule.

2. The couple came to the fertility seminar with a "What have we got to lose?" mentality. They sat in the front row, and the woman cried for most of the talk. The speaker encouraged them not only to remain hopeful, but also to spend time around families with children and to envision themselves with their own brood. They had their first baby within the following year.

3. When the banker asked for a meeting with her boss to discuss why she wasn't recommended for the promotion, the shocked supervisor said she had no idea that the part-time employee wanted to start working full-time. The banker was promoted within the year.

4. Not only did Kevin Smith not take the teacher's keys, he turned out to be one of the teacher's favorite students, ending the semester with a B+.

5. The gentleman decided to try and catch a flight from the 'wrong' airport. The airline agents were able to get him on a plane leaving at about the same time. The only seat left was in first class, which was assigned to him at no extra charge.

6. The branch manager for the financial institution refused to give into discouragement, and prayed for the woman every day. Two weeks after taking the money, the woman came back into the bank and made full restitution.

7. After the second Thursday without a response, the radio talent-wanna-be wrote a note to the producer, stating that she was going to call in two days to find out why she had not been contacted. "Whatever the reason, please just tell me the truth," the note read. When she called, the producer was extremely apologetic. "We lost your phone number!" The woman started singing jingles the following week.

8. When the cast list was posted, the young man who had not been called back discovered he had the lead part. The director explained that there had been no reason to call him back. He was so strong, there was no competition for his role.

9. The woman returned to the class later and explained that as she listened to the trainer, she realized she was rescuing her boyfriend. She had to call her mother immediately to change her instructions from, "Give him the $250 in the envelope," to "Hide the envelope!"

The unthankful heart... discovers no mercies;
but the thankful heart... will find,
in every hour, some heavenly blessings.

Henry Ward Beecher

▶ THE MIRACULOUS MUNDANE

Did you expect the miracle? Or one even better than what actually happened? If not, no need to be frustrated. Just be grateful for the awareness that it is a habit you can develop.

In the first edition of this book this chapter was entitled "Expect the Best." Certainly, there couldn't be anything better than the best, right? Yet time and time again I saw instances where people would, in the name of 'being positive', script experiences so tightly that there was no room for delight or surprise.

Beware lest your expectations become pre-meditated resentments.

Not long ago I was fortunate to sing at a wedding presided over by a good friend of mine. In his sermon, he shared that he had recently led a family reunion retreat weekend. (What a neat concept!) His first question for the couples was as follows:

"What, other than your spouse, has been your greatest disappointment in marriage?" The laughter was loud and long from the congregation.

When various Eastern philosophies invite us to have no expectations, they are setting before us the ideal. I am not there very often. I can occasionally have no expectations of my daughter doing her chores, or drivers using their turn signals, but most of the time I do struggle with specific expectations.

When one's expectations are reduced to zero,
one really appreciates everything.

Stephen Hawking

In order to keep each thought positive even when I'm not yet enlightened enough to have no expectations, I expect a miracle. That way, if something does happen that 'looks' wrong to my eyes, I can think, "Hmmm, I'm sure there's a miracle waiting in the wings behind this door!" And there is, every time.

I have watched how often we think we know what the best is... and boy, are we wrong! When we expect a miracle — it could really be spelled MYRACLE, because there is a mystery hidden within — it will be beyond our most beautiful dreams if we will only allow it to come through.

The expectations where we have settled on a pre-ordained outcome are the ones that are dangerous to our health and happiness. I remember one man not only affirming that he would become rich, but which famous person would discover him at which restaurant, etc. It was as though his life was on hold until The Moment arrived. Rather than thinking we can decide how the stars will best turn in their orbits, I much prefer staying open to what Deepak Chopra calls, "the field of endless possibilities."

That is why the universal prayer of surrender is, "Thy will be done." We simply learn to intend a completely positive result and then release the outcome to everyone's highest good.

> *I'm in love with the potential of miracles.*
> *For me, the safest place is out on a limb.*
>
> Shirley MacLaine

Just yesterday afternoon, as I was picking my daughter up from driver's ed, someone ran a red light and turned right in front of us. "Why do you think that just happened?" I asked her.

"Because of our negative thoughts?"

"Most likely, and because of my lack of positive thoughts. I didn't specifically intend and expect a wonderful, safe and enjoyable trip today. So now, let's be grateful for the reminder that our thoughts create our reality and intend a miracle." She agreed.

Within one block a van was waiting to turn into traffic. I motioned him to go ahead of us while we were stopped at a light. Then my daughter said, "Look, Mom. It's that guy from the recording studio!" Sure enough, I had been meaning to call the city's largest studio to book a time to begin recording my new original music CD. Here was my reminder staring at me. All the good feelings of how much I love music began to flood through me. It was our 'miracle'.

I could have 'expected' to see that studio producer, but it was much more fun allowing the Source of All Love and Joy to surprise me. To Expect the Best still gives me the work of picturing a 'best'. My preferred task is to be in anticipation of a miracle, and then allow life to unfold as a divine surprise each day.

▶ DESIRE, THEN RETIRE

Optimism is a fairly simple process of changing our thinking to expect a miracle, and then to release and allow. Yet, pessimism is still popular in modern society. Some people blame it on their childhood saying, "It's how I was raised." Others are now claiming a genetic predisposition to pessimism. Notice the helplessness? It is pessimistic to believe that a negative event's effect has to last forever, or a gene can control your outlook on life.

Some people blame their pessimism on the media. It's true the media focuses on the negative. Yet why is the media so attentive to bad news? Because that's what we buy and watch. Study after study has shown that newspapers featuring negative headlines sell up to 10 times as many copies as positive ones.

E Expect a Miracle

Once, while visiting my parents in Fort Myers, Florida, the evening News-Press headline read, "Pessimism Kills Heart Patients." The newspaper could have bannered, "Optimism Saves Lives" but it would have sold fewer copies.

Perhaps we fill our heads with potential catastrophes to ensure that we are prepared for all the bad things that might happen. One attraction is that expecting the worst protects us from disappointment. However, our expectations often become self-fulfilling prophecies. The good news is we can teach ourselves to expect miracles.

The human body tends to move in the direction of its expectations
– plus or minus. It is important to know that attitudes
of confidence are no less a part of the treatment program
than medical science and technology.

Dr. Norman Cousins, M.D.

▶ How To Stay Optimistic

In order to stay optimistic, I follow these basic patterns:

1. I monitor my thoughts and self-talk.

2. I strengthen my 'hope-muscles' each week by listening to and reading stories of over-comers who beat the odds.

3. I choose friends and co-workers to talk with who are upbeat and focused on staying positive.

4. I take risks and ask for what I want. When I am feeling pessimistic, I simply dare life to give me the best. I might go to a party even though I'm afraid it will be dull, and then be delightfully surprised. Life itself helps me become optimistic once again.

If you don't have confidence, get off your rear
and do anything that will make you feel better about yourself.

Dr. Wayne Dyer

We don't always get what we deserve, but we almost always get what we expect. It's time we each decide to move away from straining our brain with fear towards training our brain to expect a miracle. We can choose to use the power of positive self-fulfilling prophecies to forecast a future full of promise.

Everything that is done in the world
is done by hope.

Martin Luther

(F) Feel All Your Feelings

The young man who has not wept is a savage,
and the old man who will not laugh is a fool.

George Santayana

How important are feelings? They are the primary reason we have a job, or marry, or read a book. Ultimately, our goal in life is to feel good — joy — and to help others feel good. Life is all about feelings.

Yet sometimes, in an effort to feel good, we spend our entire lives running from feeling bad. We need to remember that we cannot experience the good feelings without allowing ourselves to feel the painful emotions. The suppression of one feeling tends to decrease feelings in general.

Think about a relationship. The only way you can guarantee you will not be hurt is not to care about the other person. As soon as you care, if the person moves to another city, you will feel the pain of sadness and loneliness. Similarly, if you never feel anger when a friend is being belittled, then you have already cut yourself off from caring about him or her.

Next think about the dreams we've talked about. If you never allow yourself to get excited, you'll never be disappointed, but you'll also never be happy and fulfilled.

Feelings are all intertwined.

When I asked a successful children's therapist what he believed was the most important message for me to share with kids, he said, "Tell them to feel all their feelings." The natural response to such a mission is, "Why would we need to teach them to feel? Isn't feeling something children do naturally?"

The answer is yes, children do feel their feelings naturally...until they are taught to do otherwise. For various reasons, as we were growing up, many of us were taught to shut off from our emotions. When we were hurting or upset, we were told to "forget it," "don't worry about it," or that we "shouldn't feel that way." Even when I speak to children today, I continue to hear that they have been taught a fear and distrust of feelings.

It is natural that we don't want to get stuck in a mad or a sad place, for both are painful. But not to feel them at all is similar to saying, "I don't want to go into a coma, so I will never shut my eyes to sleep." Healthy living requires both sleeping and allowing all our feelings.

Even the cry from the depths is an affirmation.

Martin Marty

▶ THE FEELINGS CLASS

In a short talk to a class of second-graders, I asked them a question that had no correct answer. "Would you help me list the good and bad feelings?" Knowing that feelings are neither good nor bad, I simply wanted to hear their perceptions.

Not surprisingly, they had no trouble naming the feelings they were "not supposed to feel." The emotions they all agreed to put into this negative category were 'sad' and 'mad'. I then told the children a 'what if' story.

"Let's imagine I'm a fairy godmother who can make these 'bad' feelings go away. All you have to do is ask me. But before you decide to do that, let's imagine one more thing. Let's say I take your anger away, and tomorrow is show and tell day when you've decided to take your new puppy to school.

"Recess is right before show and tell, so you take your puppy out onto the playground. Suddenly, the fourth-grade bully walks up and starts teasing you as he pulls the puppy's tail. Then he grabs the puppy right out of your hands and throws it up in the air. The puppy is crying because it's so scared. What are you going to do?"

"Stop him!" "Go get help!" "Tell him to stop!" I hear from the kids.

"But wait, you aren't even angry, remember? I took away all your anger the day before, so this wouldn't even bother you, right?"

After a moment of stunned silence, I ask if anyone wants to keep his or her anger. They all do. I ask them, "Who do we need to protect with our anger energy every day?".

"Me."

Anger is energy for protection or energy for change. I call it "Angergy." The kids catch on quickly. With adults it sometimes takes longer.

> *Action is the antidote to despair.*
> Joan Baez

I learned a lot about anger energy when I was in counseling right after my divorce. "Mary Kay, why are you smiling while you describe all these painful events?" my counselor asked during one of my sessions.

"Am I smiling? It must be because I've forgiven him."

"No," she said calmly. "You can't forgive something until you've faced it, and you are just beginning to face what has happened. Go home and write down every abusive incident from the past six years."

Eleven single-spaced pages later, I was no longer smiling. I got in touch with my repressed anger and was amazed at its power. I had so much energy that I walked for at least an hour every day. I've never been in such great physical shape as during that year of working out my anger.

> *The best patients are very open about their anxiety, hostility,*
> *their emotions in general...*
> *Whenever a nurse tells me a patient is a nuisance*
> *who keeps questioning everything. I respond,*
> *"Good, he's going to live longer."*
> Dr. Bernie Siegel, M.D.

Feel All Your Feelings

▶ DEPRESSION AND RAGE

The clinical definition of depression is anger turned inward. It is obvious that depression results in a lack of energy, while rage is the release of pent-up energy. When we repress our anger, we have no energy, or explode inappropriately.

One of the main reasons women become depressed more often that men is that women are often unwittingly taught that if they get in touch with their anger, they'll have to wear a black pointed hat for the rest of their lives. The good news is that more and more women are now realizing that anger is a healthy emotion which everyone needs to feel and release.

"I was afraid I'd turn into one of those 'itch' words: witch or the other one..."

"But what if my anger turns into rage?" I hear this from both men and women. I simply share that my ex-husband's program for recovery was similar to mine: to get in touch with his anger. Learning to notice, feel and express anger is vital to keeping depression and rage in check.

▶ THE MAD-SAD CYCLE

"I can feel mad, but I just don't do the sad thing. Too much of a downer." Years ago the person saying this in one of my audiences would have been a male. Not so today. Both genders can get caught in the SAD-FREE zone. Unfortunately, as with every imbalance such as this, there is a dear price to pay.

The reason John or Jonetta have decided they don't want to go to the Sad side of the coin is because they fear getting stuck in sadness, which society also refers to as depression. Yet it is that very fear that gets them stuck in their Anger side. Usually this stuckness plays out as rage. When we do not allow a flow from mad to sad, we tend to sink into rage.

The same holds true for the individual who simply 'doesn't do Anger'. (See the ☺ smile?) Afraid of getting stuck in anger, they instead get stuck in sadness until it acts out as depression. The healthier you are, the more you will experience a wide range of emotions; emotions that will be in-motions, passing as quickly as they came.

Take a look at your life over the past few weeks. If you're like most people, you have been stuck in either the rage of avoiding sadness or the depression of avoiding anger.

Ask yourself: Which am I seeing more often in myself?

_____

_____

_____

▶ A TON OF BRICKS

Think of an anger-event as a brick. When an upsetting situation occurs, it is often caused by someone 'crossing our boundaries'. Our feelings of anger tell us we are threatened, which we are not, but while we feel threatened, we need to set a clear boundary.

Now suppose the person we need to communicate with is our supervisor, and we have the distinct impression that even the gentlest communication of our boundary will result in the loss of our job. The result might be that our brick of anger, rather that being shared at the time, becomes stored in our rage bag.

Ragers tend to hold things in and then throw their emotional bag of bricks onto another person's head over fairly minor issues. Had the rager caught their feelings or dealt with each upset individually, he or she could have consciously handled the incident. Rage is never a conscious choice. At our house we call it, "our Bulldog."

▶ CATCHING THE BULLDOG

When I heard Eckhart Tolle speak a few years ago, I was amazed at his description of how he reacted to negative events. "I almost get giddy," he shared at the seminar. What he told the group that day dramatically affected myself and my family.

He described a 'pain body' within most of us that is the physical energy of childhood wounds. He noted that some of us have larger pain bodies, some of us have more active pain bodies, but almost all of us have one, until we learn a healing process.

In order to share this concept with my kids, I called it "our Bulldog." Translating Tolle's teaching, it came out this way:

"Usually, our bulldog is asleep, but even a bear in hibernation gets hungry eventually. Well, when the bulldog wakes up, he goes looking for food, but the only food he can eat is pain — his own and that of other people.

"He starts in our stomach, and we get a kind of uneasy feeling. Then he moves into our throat, and we start sniping a little at other people, hoping to create some food to eat.

"If we don't catch him, he'll go on up into our brain and take it over. That's when we do and say really mean things that we don't even intend. Then the Bulldog gets full on all that pain, and goes back down to our stomachs to sleep again."

"So, how do we catch him?" My 9-year old was all ears.

"Oh, with a flashlight!" (Awareness) "Bulldogs hate the light and if we shine even a little light on him by thinking or saying, 'There's my Bulldog waking up!' he'll go back to sleep."

I added one more concept from Tolle's theory:

"Now here's the really good news. Every time we catch him with the spotlight, we keep him from eating. That means he gets skinnier and skinnier. Some people get so good at catching their Bulldog before he gets to their brain, that eventually the Bulldog disappears!"

So, at our house, you may hear an occasional 'Bulldog' warning as one of us picks up on another's rising frustrations. There are many days we don't 'catch' the bulldog in time, but the times he is caught are becoming more and more frequent. It is a process that, as

Feel All Your Feelings (F)

Tolle says, almost makes you giddy. Why? Because pain is just energy, and that can be transformed to positive uses.

> *Everything is shown up by being exposed to the light,*
> *and whatever is exposed to the light itself becomes light.*
>
> Ephesians 5:13

Tolle even offers hope for women PMSers! In his book, *The Power of Now,* he offers the following,

"If you are able to stay alert and present at the time (preceding your menstrual cycle) and watch whatever you feel within, rather than be taken over by it, it affords an opportunity for the most powerful spiritual practice, and a rapid transmutation of all past pain becomes possible."

It almost makes a woman look forward to that time! (I said 'almost.')

▶ REFRAMING ANGER

One wonderful advantage of feeling our feelings is that once we see our anger, we can make choices about it. While we are in denial of our anger, it has a hold on us like a vise grip. Once we sense our own anger, we can look to the sponsoring thoughts.

We have already mentioned the concept of projection. It plays an important part here. My closest friends and I will listen when one of us is in an anger space about someone or something, and then find a time to gently ask, "Is there anyway this is your mirror?" Since we know that all life around us is a mirror of what is within us, the person feeling the anger can almost always admit that, yes, there is a reflection going on.

If you spot it, you got it.

If, for example, we are upset about someone not being open, once we can see that there are areas of *our lives* where we are not completely forthright, then we can, as Proust says, "see with new eyes." Compassion and understanding of the person we were just lashing out at comes more quickly and easily from this place of self-responsibility.

No matter what words anyone has said to you,
they were only saying two things,
"I love you" or "I'm scared. Please help me."

Get in touch with an issue that's been upsetting you lately, get out a piece of paper or a tape recorder and answer this question: "How do I feel?" "How else do I feel?"

Then keep answering over and over: "How else does it feel?" or "How else do I feel?"

Keep writing until you feel a shift in how you feel or a release of energy.

_____

_____

_____

_____

_____

_____

_____

_____

_____

► AM I MY FEELINGS?

We are not our feelings. As author Anthony De Mello, S.J., wrote in his book *Awareness*, "We are the sky. Our feelings are in the clouds," Therefore, I discourage the use of phrases such as, "I *am* angry right now." The more accurate phrase would be, "I *feel* pretty angry right now."

Our brain listens to how we phrase such descriptions of our emotional well being. Feelings of anger or frustration are temporary signals that an imbalance has occurred. Acknowledging them simply helps us to get back into balance. Granted, there are days we feel 'overcast', but we can only deal with one cloud at a time.

► A CRY FOR HELP

The other most suppressed feeling is sadness, which in the past, men tended to suppress more often than women. "Wimp!" and "Cry-baby!" are just two of the labels society uses to belittle those who allow themselves to cry. Yet crying is one of our primary mechanisms for releasing tension.

Mad and sad are two sides of the same emotional coin. Every event that we feel angry about is one that we also feel some sadness over, and vice-versa. The goal is to feel both sides of the coin. Then our sads and mads won't overwhelm us.

If a person can say, 'I don't feel anything',
Then he has cut off from feeling his own aliveness.
This statement is heard from those who are clinically depressed.

Alexander Lowen, M.D.

We cry not only when we feel desperate, but when our desperation lifts. A mother who cannot locate her child does not cry while she is frantically searching for him, but only after she has found him. A dear friend of mine shared with me that she wept deeply the first time she and her husband made love. She had connected with the child inside her and with a lost feeling of pure joy.

When my son was three, he would often ask why I was crying during times of joy. I said I was letting go of my 'happy tears'. One day, while watching a happy ending of a movie with me, he became very excited. "Look, Mom!" he exclaimed as he pointed to his cheeks, "I have happy tears now, too!"

Ask yourself: "If someone referred to me as 'emotional,' how would I choose to respond?"

_____

_____

_____

_____

"Am I uncomfortable sharing my feelings or having others share their feelings with me?"

_____

_____

I recently heard someone remark, "People are emotionally constipated!" I chuckled, but I had to agree. One reason we are so emotionally repressed could be because of the painful experiences of our great-great grandparents. In the early days of this nation, all families lost children to death on a regular basis. Their allotted time for grieving was sometimes half an hour before the wagon train moved on, or before the plantation master returned home. Family members had to suppress their emotions in order to survive.

Whatever reasons people used to have for shutting down emotionally, they no longer exist. It's time we allowed ourselves to *feel* better.

▶ THE MAN WHO DARED NOT CRY

After my divorce, I participated in a weekend retreat for divorced, separated and widowed singles. While the other six members of my small group and I cried freely, one very solidly built farmer in his early 30's remained silent and did not shed a tear — until the last day.

We were invited to write good-bye letters to our former spouses to gently close the door on our past. Then, anyone who wanted to read his or her letter was invited to do so. One by one, in powerful sharing, everyone in the group read their letters except the young farmer. Courageously, the facilitator asked if he, too, would like to read the letter he held in his hand.

(F) Feel All Your Feelings

I then witnessed something that left a great impression on me. This huge man, whose body was as rigid as a cement block, began to crumble. At first, he just choked, as the frightened part of him struggled to hold back the emotions that another part of him was straining to release. Two group members ran to hold him as he shook violently. Finally, his huge chest, perhaps so large because it had held so much for so long, began to heave in convulsing sobs.

As he wept violently, he told us he worked on a farm with his father. He shared that his two-year-old daughter had died three years before, and that his father's response to any mention of the little girl's name had always been to look down at the ground.

"I started to do the same thing whenever my wife would talk about her. It's no wonder she left me. I shut down my heart to any feelings," he poured out to us. He then read us a good-bye letter, not to his wife — he said that would come later — but to his little girl.

I have always felt sorry for people afraid of feeling, of sentimentality,
who are unable to weep with their whole hearts.

Golda Meir

▶ No Tears Allowed

Anyone who watched the '96 Olympics in Atlanta might recall a painful scene.

19-year-old Shannon Miller, with one small mistake, slipped from medal contention to a distant tenth place in the women's individual gymnastics standings. TV viewers listened in as the coach of the extremely young team exhorted her to stop crying. "Suck it up!" he exclaimed to the young woman whose dreams had just come crashing down. His words were one more indictment against the 'sin' of crying.

"How are you feeling?" we ask someone who is recovering from an illness. It is time we ask ourselves *how we are feeling our feelings.* At this point in history, the only thing that is keeping us from experiencing all of our feelings is our fear of them. It's time we allow our children and ourselves to answer, "I'm feeling (my feelings) really well."

Take a moment to affirm your ability and desire to feel the side of the emotional coin that you have been shunning. One simple refrain such as, "I honor my (anger or sadness) as sacred," written out or repeated can free us up to start 'feeling better'.

Ask yourself: What words would best affirm my emotional self and free me to be happier and healthier?

_____

_____

_____

_____

Feel All Your Feelings

▶ GETTING INTO THE FLOW

One of most amazing simple techniques to help us feel our feelings is to breathe deeply. Dr. Lowen says "to breath deeply is to feel deeply."

Often we busy ourselves to the point that we remark we "barely have time to breathe." When Lowen had patients who were suppressing a feeling, they were usually holding their breath. The simple instruction to breathe helped release their emotions.

Body-Mind author Louise L. Hay suggests a similar technique when dealing with fear: "When you get scared, become aware of your breath as it flows in and out of your body. Recognize that your breath, this most precious substance, is freely given to you. You have enough to last for as long as you live. Take a deep breath, go within and understand that life will support you in whatever way you need it to."

Other techniques I find helpful when I'm feeling mad or sad:

1. Check my comments for sarcasm (anger that isn't getting validated)
2. Check for a lump in my throat or for a scratchy throat
3. Beat a pillow, stamp my feet, or throw eggs at trees
4. Journal anything and everything that comes to mind
5. Take a walk
6. Express aloud to my friend the feelings that come to me. I ask him or her to "hold a space for me." We do not analyze, judge, or try to 'fix' my feelings. I am simply allowed to give them a voice.
7. Rent a sad movie (*An Affair to Remember* or *My Life* are two of my favorites)
8. Start or join a support group such as a 12-step Emotions Anonymous
9. Seek out a good therapist and or body-worker
10. Spend an afternoon with children

Here is an interesting game for all ages:

Write 20 different feelings on slips of paper.

Put the 20 slips in an envelope.

One person pulls out a feeling word and reads it aloud.

Everyone in the group shares a time when he or she felt that feeling.

When all have shared, someone else pulls out another slip of paper, and the game continues.

This game can lead to discussions of such topics as what we do when we feel certain feelings, how what we think affects what we feel, and how all feelings are temporary.

▶ FEELINGS AS SENSING

Every emotion is a feeling, but not every feeling is an emotion. Some feelings are more like sensations. Intuition is a kind of sensing feeling that everyone possesses to some degree. Once discovered, it can greatly enrich our lives.

The founder of Sony was asked by author Deepak Chopra how he became so financially successful without ever taking any business courses. Chopra was told, "I swallow the deal. If it gives me indigestion, I don't sign it."

There are three signs of intuition. The first is that my thought is not rational. It does not make logical sense. Second, it will repeat itself. The irrational thought will return after I've dismissed it as 'silly'. Finally, true intuition is always rooted in love and would never encourage hurtful behaviors.

Record a time when you felt something in your gut.

_____

_____

_____

_____

_____

_____

_____

_____

When we 'go with the flow' of our feelings, we experience a sense of relief, a connectedness with life, a deeper understanding of others and ourselves and greater acceptance and love. We cannot be free until we are free to feel.

To feel is to heal.

Eddy Buchanan

F

Feel All Your Feelings

Gratitude and Appreciation

Gratitude and Appreciation

You'll never meet a happy ungrateful person,
or an unhappy grateful person.

Zig Ziglar

Gratitude costs nothing but can yield the greatest rewards. In our homes, workplaces and schools, moments of gratitude and appreciation are small seeds that can become mighty oaks.

Many parents in my seminars complain that their children are ungrateful. I ask, "Do your children see parents who are grateful?" The answer is, not often enough.

Whether it's for babies, beauty or other blessings...Gratitude is our natural state. When we release fears of tomorrow and regrets of yesterday, we stand in awe at the fullness of the present moment. *If you are looking for one word to sum up the essence of positive attitude, joy, or peace, you will find it in gratitude.*

It is both energizing and healing to focus on what we are grateful for. Simply by moving into a thought of appreciation, you can make the difference between attracting love and attracting judgment. Gratitude is the easiest way to raise your Score and thus your level of happiness.

Often, a heightened sense of gratitude comes only after a loss. We lose a child, a sibling, a parent or a friend and are much more appreciative of our loved ones remaining. We can learn about the importance of gratitude from wisdom or from woe. Wisdom is the easier path.

▶ WHO IS GRATEFUL?

I find that the teachers best able to teach me about gratitude fall into three categories:

1. Those who have experienced a loss
2. Those who have come very close to a loss
3. Those who know a loss is coming

▶ Those Who Have Experienced a Loss

One of my gratitude teachers was a man named Jim. One afternoon he shared this story with me:

"When I was in the war, survival and sanity were daily battles. One night as I was trying to sleep, I became greatly disturbed by the fact that my socks were wet. Amid the awfulness, this discomfort began to gnaw at me. I remember going to sleep that night promising God that if I could ever again go to sleep with dry socks on, I would be forever grateful."

When Jim survived the war, he kept his promise in the form of a daily gratitude list. Each night before retiring, he wrote out those things he was grateful for.

At the age of 57, Jim was happily married and owner of a thriving business. Then calamity struck. His major supplier went bankrupt. Jim lost the business as well as the beautiful home in the country that had been his wife's dream all their married life.

"Often times, the only thing on my gratitude list was "dry socks," but it got me through those hard times," Jim shared. "It's the reason I am alive today."

He who receives a benefit with gratitude,
repays the first installment on his debt.
Seneca

When I had the opportunity to interview author Nathaniel Branden in 1993, I saw a picture of his wife on his desk and commented on her beauty. His face lit up as he described her as "one of most consistently happy people I have ever known." In explaining what set her apart, Branden noted, "In the darkest days of her life, she learned gratitude. She almost never goes to sleep without taking time to review everything good in her life; these are typically her last thoughts of the day."

A few minutes spent in total awe will contribute to your
spiritual awakening more than any metaphysics course.
Dr. Wayne Dyer

▶ Those Who Have Come Close to a Loss
A year after his heart attack, a gentleman in his 60's was asked by our local paper to describe the greatest change in his life during those twelve months. Without hesitation he said, "My attitude." The reporter asked for an example of what that change looked like.

"Now I have the gratitude attitude," the man replied. "Like, this morning I was out jogging, saw some friends sitting on the porch, waved at them, and said, 'Great day to be above ground, isn't it?'"

My best friend was another who experienced a brush with potential loss. On a particular Saturday morning, she was ecstatic. She had just bought a cabin on a nearby lake, fulfilling one of her dreams. As she drove there that day, her mind was churning with plans of how she would fix it up and make it her own. She does not remember hearing or seeing anything to alarm her... until she was in the middle of four railroad tracks.

"I'm not sure why the arm didn't go down to signal that a train was coming. I only know that the engineer and I looked each other in the eye we were so close." When she reached the other side, barely missing a collision, her eyes filled with tears of gratitude. Every breath she took that day reminded her of her gift of life.

▶ Those Who Know a Loss is Coming
From his diagnosis with cancer in January to his passing in March, my father was one of the most grateful people I have ever encountered. The stern perfectionist was transformed into a gentle cheerleader by the news that his time with us might be cut short.

Every sunset, every song, every person who walked into the room was a tremendous gift which he unwrapped with care. This man loved dancing and I remember the last time I saw him out of a wheelchair. The med-tech was walking him and his pole full of tubes back from the restroom when he stopped her, "Wait!" he said smiling, "They're playing our song!" and he put his arm around her waist and moved her gracefully from side to side.

Gratitude and Appreciation **G**

We do not need a crisis to pull us into gratitude, just a decision. When we tire of being tired and are bored of feeling bored, all we need do is open our awareness to the marvelous miracle before us, which is this moment.

For it is written that on judgment day a man shall be asked
of every good thing that he saw and did not enjoy.

The Talmud

1. On a scale of 1–10, how grateful and appreciative am I lately?

_____

2. What are 5 things I am grateful for from the past 24 hours?

_____

_____

_____

_____

_____

▶ How to Go GA-GA

The goal of every moment of my life these days is to go GA-GA: *to be in Gratitude and Appreciation of every experience before me and within me.* I cannot tell you what life will be like when I get to such a constant state of appreciation, but I can tell you that every day's progress feels better than the day before.

"But how can I be grateful for the life/marriage/job/illness that I have now?" the questions pop up. Just today I heard my teenager wail, "It's hard to be grateful all the time!" I reminded her that if someone were holding us hostage until we could come up with something to be grateful for, we would have no difficulty finding it, so rather than hold joy and prosperity hostage, it is worth striving for gratitude.

Yes, there is Nirvanah:
it is in leading your sheep to a green pasture,
and in putting your child to sleep, and in writing the last line of your poem.

Kahlil Gibran

Each of us can discipline ourselves to see what we appreciate as easily as we can learn to inhale that next wonderful breath of fresh air. Gratitude is natural. It is just a matter of getting back into the habit of doing it.

Why make the effort? Because the feeling of gratitude brings a fountain of joy to every moment where it is invited in. According to stress specialist Hans Selye, "Gratitude is the most important of all human emotions." Meanwhile it causes a ripple effect that is a source of love and abundance not only in our lives, but also in the lives of those we live and work with. The ramifications of this seemingly small and insignificant activity are unbelievably powerful.

For those of you who are especially challenged by the concept of being grateful for everyone and everything in every moment, don't start with your in-laws or your former boss. Start with something very simple.

> *Most of us miss out on life's big prizes. The Pulitzer, The Nobel.*
> *Oscars. Tonys. Emmys. But we're all eligible for life's small pleasures.*
> *A pat on the back. A kiss behind the ear. A four-pound bass. A full moon.*
> *An empty parking space. A crackling fire. A great meal. A glorious sunset.*
> *Hot soup. Cold beer. Don't fret about copping life's grand awards.*
> *Enjoy its tiny delights. There are plenty for all of us.*

United Technologies Corporation ad

I find the best times to Go GA-GA are in the morning when I awaken, at the end of my day, or at mealtimes. My children and I are not always the best at rituals, but we do remember 99% of the time to say thanks before each meal. When I invite those joining us for meals to give thanks, I remind them that we can thank our higher power, but we can also be grateful for the waitress, the cook, the farmer, or the chicken who gave her life so that we might have such wonderful nourishment! Giving thanks is, in and of itself, a blessing!

▶ EVERY DAY IS CHRISTMAS DAY

▶ Go to a Gratitude Place in Your Mind:

Imagine yourself alone in an empty room. There is nothing on the walls, not even a ticking clock. Just you, sitting on your chair, waiting. Suddenly, the door opens, and people you have never met before start to bring in boxes and set them before you.

"These gifts just arrived for you," the last one says, as he closes the door behind him. Then, one by one, you sit and open the gifts that are in your life right now. You have never seen them before and they amaze you. From the child who makes you smile, to the friend who confides in you, to the talent you have that others do not, to the squirrel that plays in your front yard. For hours that turn into days, you open your gifts.

Some of the thoughts and feelings you experienced as you went to your Gratitude Place:

_____

_____

_____

"Stop and smell the roses" is a common refrain in our busy times, reminding us to look with fresh eyes at what is. We teach young children to label rather than appreciate. "That is a tree," we say. Therefore, all trees are logged into our computer brains and we are no longer touched by the experience of the young sapling or the mighty maple. The result, far from gratitude, is a kind of boredom or restlessness that misses that something 'out there' that we are looking for.

It is here, in the moment, that all perfection resides. When we choose to allow ourselves to be embraced by it, we see the miracle that is all life and are enveloped in awe and appreciation.

Just to be is a blessing. Just to live is holy.
Abraham Heschel

Since my high school teaching days, I have exhorted seekers to walk outside and get to know a living creation in nature. It's your turn...

Find a tree, bush, flower or blade of grass and be with it. Let it teach you, quiet you, or comfort you. Take three deep breaths as you gently put aside any resistance to this as being 'silly'. Spend at least five minutes in contemplation with your new friend. When your experience is complete, write your insights here:

_____

_____

_____

_____

_____

_____

_____

_____

_____

_____

_____

▶ GIFT FROM THE GEESE

It was early one holiday morning. The kids were still in bed. I had awakened early to get some more writing in. After two hours of focused work I decided I was done for the day. I wasn't quite where I had set my goal for that morning, but I was 'close enough'.

Just then, I heard the honking. Geese were flying somewhere overhead. "Wish I could see them," I thought, "but by the time I get outside to see where they are..." Just then, they flew directly into my line of vision through the small window in front of me. "You can do it!" they honked to their leader. "Don't give up, we're behind you all the way!" (That is the reason geese honk, to encourage.) I dug in and met my goal for the day.

Whom do I thank for support throughout this book project? Nothing less than all that is. These pages cannot hold my gratitude.

> *Why do some people always see beautiful skies and grass*
> *and lovely flowers and incredible human beings,*
> *while others are hard-pressed to find anything or any place that is beautiful?*
>
> Leo Buscaglia

▶ GRATITUDE IN THE WORKPLACE

What would our lives be like if we made a commitment to gratitude? On a professional level, gratitude could make an impact more significantly positive than the introduction of computers. At a major corporation, one of my classes decided to look at the results of a recent "greatest needs" survey. *The need for recognition* topped the employees' needs list at the plant, as it does at most workplaces.

As our group discussed what could be done to address the problem, their first thoughts were to chastise those supervisors who were not recognizing the achievements of their team members. Slowly it dawned on the class that they were doing the very thing they were condemning: finding fault rather than appreciating. Thus, they came up with creative ways to recognize those individuals in the plant who were recognizing others.

The first person they decided to share their gratitude with was their CEO, a man they greatly admired as an individual and a leader. They discussed which method to use, and the idea of a green philodendron plant symbolizing the "growing plant" won approval. "But what if he gets dozens of plants as gifts?" one gentleman asked. He then volunteered to contact the executive's secretary to see if that was the case.

What was reported back stunned the group. "Not only has he never received a plant or any gift from anyone here at the site these past five years, but when I went to see his secretary, she pulled out the only thank-you note she'd ever received. It was sent to her three years ago, and she's kept it all this time," the team member shared. "The people at the top don't get the recognition they deserve either."

The group also decided to make a video of "Moments of Great Recognition" to share with the CEO and the training department. In the video, one woman, who had been at the plant for over 25 years, shared that one of her happiest memories was the day her supervisor brought sugar-free cookies to a party, because she knew this woman was diabetic — a small but significant gesture.

Gratitude and Appreciation **G**

Blessed are those who can give without remembering,
and take without forgetting.

Princess Bibesco

▶ THREE STEPS FOR SHOWING APPRECIATION

Remember the steps for asking for what you want that were covered in Habit A: "When you," "I feel," "Because?" The first three of the steps are a beautiful way to show gratitude as well.

Recently, I worked on this skill with a group of surgical technicians from area hospitals. After I had taught the process, I asked for a volunteer to take the risk of using the first three of the four steps to thank someone present that day at the seminar.

A woman stood and said, "Marilyn, do you have a minute?

1. When you encouraged me just now at break to consider a nursing career,

2. I felt really good, and very grateful,

3. Because it means you've been noticing my extra efforts and interest. I just wanted you to know how much I appreciated your comments."

Her taking the risk to share her sentiments in front of all of us stands out in my memory as the most powerful moment of that day.

Silent gratitude isn't much use to anyone.

Gladys Borwyn Stern

Another habit I encourage in the workplace is regular RAVEing. A RAVE is a way of **R**ecognizing **A**nd **V**aluing **E**mployees/**E**mployers. The formula is simple: Simply choose 3–5 qualities from the following list to put on a thank you note. The note could read something like this:

Hello, _____!

I just wanted to write a quick note and let you know some of the things I admire about you! You are _____, _____ and _____.

These are all qualities I value highly, just as I value you! Thanks for sharing your gifts!

Signed,

_____

▷ **QUALITIES WORTH PRAISING** ◁

- Able to accept constructive criticism
- Able to admit mistakes
- Able to think on your feet
- Achievement oriented
- Adventurous
- Affirming
- Ambitious
- Artistic
- Assertive
- Athletic
- Authentic
- Balanced
- Beautiful
- Bold
- Bright
- Calm
- Caring
- Charismatic
- Cheerful
- Clear thinker
- Clever
- Communicative
- Compassionate
- Concerned
- Concise
- Confident
- Congenial
- Considerate
- Consistent
- Cooperative
- Courageous
- Creative
- Curious
- Daring
- Decisive

- Deliberate
- Dependable
- Determined
- Diligent
- Diplomatic
- Down to Earth
- Dynamic
- Easy Going
- Empathetic
- Energetic
- Enterprising
- Entertaining
- Entrepreneurial
- Expressive
- Fair-minded
- Faithful
- Far-sighted
- Firm
- Focused
- Forceful
- Forgiving
- Friendly
- Fun-loving
- Funny
- Generous
- Gentle
- Genuine
- Grateful
- Great Memory
- Handsome
- Happy
- Hardworking
- Healthy
- Honest
- Humble
- Idealistic
- Independent

- Industrious
- Ingenious
- Intelligent
- Interesting
- Introspective
- Intuitive
- Kind
- Leader
- Level-headed
- Logical
- Loving
- Loyal
- Mature
- Methodical
- Motivated
- Musical
- Natural
- Objective
- Observant
- Open-minded
- Optimistic
- Organized
- Outgoing
- Passionate
- Patient
- Perceptive
- Persevering
- Persuasive
- Physically fit
- Playful
- Poised
- Proactive
- Professional
- Quick Learner
- Rational
- Reflective
- Reliable

Gratitude and Appreciation

qualities worth praising, continued

◆ Resilient	◆ Spontaneous	◆ Tough-minded
◆ Respectful	◆ Steady	◆ Trustworthy
◆ Responsible	◆ Strong-willed	◆ Unassuming
◆ Risk Taker	◆ Systematic	◆ Unpretentious
◆ Self-assured	◆ Tactful	◆ Upbeat
◆ Self-aware	◆ Talented	◆ Verbal
◆ Self-confident	◆ Team Player	◆ Versatile
◆ Self-reliant	◆ Tenacious	◆ Visionary
◆ Sense of humor	◆ Thorough	◆ Vivacious
◆ Serene	◆ Thoughtful	◆ Warm
◆ Sincere	◆ Thrifty	◆ Wise
◆ Sociable	◆ Tolerant	◆ Witty

Expressing gratitude is a simple skill, but as with all other risks, it takes courage. At one seminar I asked the audience members, "What is a risk you would like to take here at work, but haven't yet taken?"

One woman answered, "I would like to let people know how grateful I am to work here."

Gratitude is the attitude of the winners in life. "Of course," say the more cynical individuals, "I'd be grateful if I were a big winner, too." However, the winner's gratitude almost always came *before* they won. If someone is ungrateful the day before a wonderful event occurs in their life, the chance of the event transforming them is minimal.

▶ INGRAINED INGRATITUDE?

Ingratitude can have two faces. One face is indifference, or a lack of appreciation. The other face of ingratitude is compulsion, a feeling of always being 'One Short'. In the books and tapes by Abraham-Hicks, it is pointed out that we are ever swinging on a pendulum between Contentment and Desire.

Desire, as we discussed in the chapter on Habit A, is hot. It is always seeking, compelling, longing to move from what is to what could be. Desire is great, but for a joyful life it needs its counterpart. Contentment is the cool night to desire's warm day.

We have all witnessed the addictive compulsion that unbridled craving can generate. Desire and contentment work best with each other as if on a see-saw for balance and peace. Too much of either is a prescription for frustration. Our spirit longs to move back and forth to find a joyful balance.

Everyone swings back and forth between desire and contentment. Which are you stronger in right now?

What could you do to get into greater balance?

_____

_____

_____

_____

_____

_____

_____

My final recommendation for joining the Gratitude Gang is to Make Lists! Just as Nathaniel Branden's wife and Jim from the war both ended their days with gratitude lists, get in the habit of challenging yourself to come up with 10 things you are grateful for. The resulting positive attitude (or sweet dreams) will raise your Score and be a magnet for pleasant experiences in your life. Like attracts like, and as you watch for it and appreciate it, the gratitude that goes around comes around!

▶ I THANK YOU TO GO

Not long ago my kids and I took a small vacation. As we pulled out of the driveway, we chatted about the importance of going GA-GA to attract the best people and experiences for our trip. That evening, as we drove into a medium-sized city fairly late, we decided we were hungry and wanted some fast food. We stopped at the next drive-through we saw and ended up in a very slow line of full cars.

"Okay," I shared with a hungry back seat. "Let's get into gratitude!" Our list was fun and made the wait seem shorter. We were grateful that:

1. There are food places open this late

2. We arrived safe and sound

3. We have a nice car with air conditioning

4. One of us was able to express his need for food

5. The sky is clear and we can see the stars through the sunroof

6. Mom's job allows us to go on vacations

7. The car that's three cars ahead of us just got their food

8. The police help keep this city safe at night

9. We have four more days of vacation

Coming up with the list ("my turn!") got a tired group into a much better feeling place. Shortly thereafter, we were up at the window.

"Thank you for being open so late," I said as I offered him my money.

But the young man declined as he handed us our sacks and drinks. "No, thank you for waiting. It's on me. Sorry for the wait!"

Make that the 10th thing we were grateful for.

▶ GRATITUDE AMONG FRIENDS

I recall a recent meeting of my women's group. We hadn't seen each other in four weeks, and there was much catching up to do. Each person who shared had faced a major challenge during our time apart, and the tears flowed. When it was time to end our sharing, there was silence, until one woman said what was in all of our hearts. "I've never had friends like this before." Our tears became tears of gratitude.

Gratitude opens the heart and bridges the gaps. It is an antidote to despair and discouragement. It is not only freeing, it is free. We need pass no new laws nor buy new books for our schools. We must simply be open to feeling it and committed to sharing it.

If the only prayer you say in your entire life is "Thank You,"
that would suffice.

Meister Eckhart

Hugs and Touch (H)

RX for indigestion, insomnia, isolation, or the blues:
One fluffy puppy — to be snuggled at meals, at bedtime or
when just home from a tough day at the office.

When life is rubbing us the wrong way, touch can get us back in touch with our healthier and happier selves. It can relax and reassure us. In addition, this basic need touches us at a very primal level. The connection between human contact and well-being is far more than skin-deep.

▶ THE BENEFITS OF TOUCH

Recent studies show a variety of benefits from touching:

1. The arteries of rabbits fed a high-cholesterol diet and petted regularly had 60% less blockage than did the arteries of unpetted but similarly fed rabbits.

2. Rats handled for 15 minutes a day during the first three weeks of their lives showed dramatically less memory loss as they grew old, compared with non-handled rats.

3. Children and adolescents hospitalized for psychiatric problems demonstrated remarkable reductions in anxiety levels, as well as positive changes in attitude, when they received a brief daily back rub.

4. Patients in nursing homes fared better when regularly hugged by their family or friends.

5. In countries where mothers work all day in the fields and carry their infants in slings, the children grow up more disease-resistant and better emotionally adjusted than those who are touched less.

6. Adults who received regular massages had reduced tension and anxiety, increased circulation, and more of the feel-good brain chemicals called 'endorphins'.

The *Touch Research Institute* in Miami and Paris has found that touch is consistently found to:

- Reduce pain
- Reduce stress hormones
- Alter the immune system
- Alleviate depressive symptoms

In addition, massage and increased touch have been shown to decrease symptoms and also sometimes speed recovery for the following:

- Asthma
- Cerebral Palsy
- HIV
- Sexual abuse
- Burns
- Diabetes
- PMS
- ADHD
- Depression
- Hypertension
- Down Syndrome
- Sleep disorder
- Chronic fatigue

Finally, TRI has found that massage also assists those dealing with:

- Smoking Cessation
- Anxiety
- Job stress
- Aggression in pre-schoolers

My favorite memories of touch would include:

_____

_____

_____

_____

_____

_____

_____

_____

Out of 100% of my need for it, the amount of touch I am receiving these days would average:

_____

▶ AFFECTION AFFECTS US

Touch heals — both individuals and relationships. In connecting us with others, touch reconnects us with an inner healing potential that is not otherwise activated. Research is beginning to bring us a clearer understanding of how healing energy is heightened through touch. For now, let's consider what happens when a four-year-old scrapes his knee.

"I fell down!" Mom hears between sobs. What the child is doing is instinctive: Placing his hand over the wound, and running to Mom to have her kiss it or touch it. Studies now indicate that Mom's hand often becomes warm to hot as she caresses the wound. "The warmth of a Mother's love," is more than just a figure of speech — as is "the heat of passion."

The leader of a Youth Program told me how one of his groups was being disrupted by two very unruly eleven-year-old boys. The problem was solved when he got the group to sit in a circle and rub each others' backs. The two had never understood before that it was possible to touch (be touched) without hurting,

So how do we incorporate the natural healing behavior of touch back into our lives? We can either reconnect with our bodies, or we can first learn to be emotionally sensitive. Our bodies will then follow suit. To be loved, we must be love-able; that is, able to love. We must learn to open our hearts and be vulnerable, emotionally as well as physically.

*Any rigidity of my body prevents me
from vibrating in resonance with others.*
Alexander Lowen, M.D.

Think of a very muscular individual with his or her arms crossed over their chests. Does this stance invite a hug? Hardly. The message is, "I do not need anyone. Stay away." A board and an iron bar cannot hug because they are too stiff. So, quite often, it is our emotional stiffness that holds us back from reaching out to others through touch. Take this quick inventory to see how emotionally flexible or rigid you tend to be:

Answer these as best you can:

How stubborn would my friends say I tend to be?

_____

_____

When I'm wrong, can I back down and apologize?

_____

_____

Can I change my mind/direction without undue embarrassment?

_____

_____

How spontaneous am I when someone proposes an outing?

_____

_____

Do I tend to get into ruts, or do I constantly and enthusiastically look for new possibilities?

_____

_____

When we care about others, as healthy individuals do, we allow ourselves to show vulnerability both emotionally and physically. Rigid bodies and hardened hearts cause physical and emotional illness.

Hugs and Touch

► THE ANTI-TOUCH TABOOS

Why don't more of us 'keep in touch'? The amount of contact with which we are comfortable may partially depend on our geographic roots. One study in the '60's noted the number of touches exchanged by people sitting in coffee shops around the world:

- In Puerto Rico, people touched each other 180 times per hour.
- In Paris, France, 110 times per hour.
- In Gainesville, Florida, two times per hour
- In London, England, according to the study, the researchers are still waiting for someone to touch their companion at a coffee shop! ☺

► CHALLENGES AND CHOICES

The anti-touch sentiment that seems to pervade our schools and workplaces has been fueled by many factors. Some of the most powerful barriers are the following:

- **Challenge:** In the past few decades many child-rearing professionals have either implied or stated outright that a baby can be spoiled by too much holding. This has resulted in infants spending hours in their cribs.

  Response: We now know that the more a baby is touched, held, and breast-fed, the healthier the baby will be, both physically and emotionally. (A 1996 study indicated that breast-feeding may also help reduce SIDS deaths.)

- **Challenge:** Many present day adults spent the first days in their lives in a crib of a hospital ward rather than in their parents' arms. This trend began with babies born in the '40's. It worsened in the '50's, when mothers were encouraged to have only occasional visits with their newborns, so they could rest. This resulted in emotional wounding, rather than the bonding so important to an infant's development.

  Response: We need to reaffirm in every way a parent's and baby's need to touch each other in the first moments, days, months, and years of the baby's life. This includes having the infant with the parent(s) in the hospital at all times, unless there is a special circumstance creating a need for separation.

- **Challenge:** Ten years ago, I heard a grandfather say to his five-year-old grandson who had just climbed excitedly onto his lap, "We don't do this anymore. You're five now." The fear of being labeled 'gay' has frightened many men and women into denying and suppressing their need for touch.

  Response: In Poland and Italy, adult women friends of all ages and sexual preferences walk the streets hand in hand and arm in arm. We must let go of "what will people think" long enough to ask what it is we want and need. Then we must trust that our inner wisdom will lead us to healthier habits of touch.

- **Challenge:** The sexual harassment cases that have received so much media attention often fail to address the lack of assertiveness on the part of the victims. Part of the problem is that women have silently put up with inappropriate behavior for too long. We need to own our responsibility in this regard.

Response: Rather than blaming others for past patterns, we can take responsibility with a phrase such as: "I helped train individuals to continue the behavior with my silence. That was then, this is now. Today I shall choose to set limits and stand by them."

- **Challenge:** Sexual misconduct with children is the most serious and dangerous touch issue. Since fewer families live in close-knit neighborhoods and small towns, we often find ourselves leaving our children with virtual strangers at day-cares, birthday parties, or scouting meetings.

  Response: Involvement with our children's friends, personal screening and strict precautions are necessary. A good friend of mine put together a social 'Lock-in' for the moms of her grade school in order to get to know them better. All the Moms arrived at 6:00 pm for a meal completely catered by their spouses. Then the men were excused, the doors locked, no emergency phone calls were allowed, and the women shared everything from crazy foolishness to quiet talks and prayer for the next 5 hours. They knew it was a huge success when the parking lots jammed for the rest of the school year with mothers exchanging greetings and information.

Finally, we must address the most unfortunate of all touch crimes — incest. From my many friends who have addressed incest in their family of origin, I have heard as much anger toward the parent who did not protect them, usually the mother, as toward the perpetrator. Moral here? Ask questions, watch for signs such as withdrawal, a change in grades, nervousness around the suspected sibling or adult, unexplained bruises and accident proneness or inconsistent moods. Sometimes the child enjoys the attention from the abuser and wants to be with him/her more than with their peers, sometimes the reverse. Refusal to 'tell' is practically universal.

Frequently the thought of incest is so horrific that families prefer to accuse the child of lying rather than confront and investigate the perpetrator. Even if the child is lying, doing so conceals a problem that needs to be addressed. When in doubt, arrange for them to speak with a professional counselor, preferably who does not know the family and is less likely to be influenced by preconceptions.

▶ TEACHERS AND TOUCHING

Can we err on the side of too much caution? I believe so. For example, once instructors are screened and deemed appropriate and fit to teach our children, we must allow them to touch those they teach. Fear of being sued is sometimes translated by wary school administrators as, 'Hands off.' If the purpose of schools is learning, we must face the fact that students learn better from teachers who touch them.

A therapist shared with me an excellent example of the touching-teaching link. His friend, also a therapist, had been working for six months with a woman and had had little success. He was considering ending their sessions, but at the following appointment he was thrilled when the woman described having accomplished the goals set for her.

"What happened to finally motivate you to do all this?" the therapist asked.

"I just did what my hair stylist suggested."

Fascinated, the therapist began to study how touch helps relax people and open them up. The results of his study were so astounding that he changed his career track. Today, he teaches therapy techniques to hair stylists all across the country.

A powerful example of our need to touch our children is contained in *Chicken Soup for the Soul, Volume I*. The story is simply called, "The Hand." It's about a kindergartner at Thanksgiving time who is asked to draw something he is grateful for. No one in the class, including the teacher, guesses what is represented by his simple drawing of a hand. It turns out, he is most grateful for the teacher who allows him to put his hand in hers at recess.

If we want to touch our children's lives, we must touch our children. Imagine a law in our schools forbidding eye contact with students. (After all, a teacher's lascivious wink to a student could harm that child for life!) We must come back to our senses — all of them.

▶ TOUCHING THROUGH HUGS

Many 'normal-looking' folks among us have been mis-touched or touch-deprived early in life. It is extremely important for us to honor our own as well as other's needs to begin touching again at out own pace. One 'touching' technique accessible to all of us is the human hug.

I'll never forget the day my former mother-in-law asked me to teach her how to hug. Her son and I had just returned from a short vacation, and I was hugging her daughter. When I greeted the older woman with a smile and a "Hello," she asked, "Why don't I ever get a hug?"

Stunned, I assured her it was not an intentional slight; I just wasn't aware that she was comfortable hugging. "I would be if someone would show me how." From that time on, we hugged. It was as simple as that.

▶ THE HAPPY HUGGER

A similar incident was responsible for winning my Dad over to hugging. Tom, a boy I dated in college, was known on campus as "The Happy Hugger." Whether with men, women, professors or janitorial staff, he spread love through hugs wherever he went.

The first time I brought Tom home to meet my parents, I failed to warn him that my 'Dr.' Dad was not of the hugging persuasion. So when we walked into my home together, Tom swept Dad off his feet with a huge bear hug. My family and I stood there, stunned and silent, as Dad, just as surprised, collected himself.

Four days later, when it was time for us to return to campus, Tom extended his hand to Dad, and was swept off his feet by hugging's newest devotee.

▶ THE HUGGING MANAGER?

I'll always remember giving my first training course for managers. It was one of my most challenging assignments. Throughout the course, three gentlemen maintained very tight and closed body language. Their arms, crossed over their chests, spoke to me of how they were protecting themselves, especially their hearts, from being touched.

I planned a special graduation ceremony for the final day of class and brought three professional massage therapists and their massage chairs with me. I tucked them all into adjoining rooms and proceeded into the classroom. After congratulating the participants on their hard work, I passed out a journaling exercise.

"I want to collect your thoughts on paper before we share them aloud," I said to the twelve who sat before me. "In addition, I have a graduation surprise. I want three of you at a time to go down the hall to receive your gift. Would you be the first?" I asked, as I gestured toward the three reticent managers.

"What is it?" asked Steve, the burliest of the group.

"It's a surprise!" the group chided. Ten minutes later, all the time needed for this form of keep-all-your-clothes-on massage, Steve returned.

"Well? How was it?" asked one the other managers.

"I don't think you're going to like it," he said to her with a smile stretching across his face. "So I'll just take your place."

The 'ice' was broken — or should I say melted — through the warmth of healing hands.

As the group left the classroom, I announced that good-bye handshakes and hugs were both available. Steve busied himself until he was the last to leave.

After a thank-you and a good-bye hug, Steve admitted, "If only I could hug my work-team, I know it would make an incredible difference."

"If you don't think people can tell the difference between a warm hug like that and a hot hug that's sexual, you're underestimating your staff," I challenged him. "You're a great hugger. Just do it."

▶ How-to-Hug

Just as the incident with my mother-in-law revealed, many people are fearful of hugging 'wrong'. There is a no real how-to for hugging, so you do not need to buy a book. Likewise, there is no particular 'when' to hug. Anytime you need a hug you can ask a friend for one. There are some 'who's' because not everyone has learned the joy of this heart-to-heart experience. Hugging doesn't work when only one party is comfortable joining in.

Where is your comfort level? One summer I did a study of 10 local churches to see how many times I was touched, from the time I walked in the door for the service to when I walked back to my car. The average was twice, once being for the collection!

Not so at our church, which recently won an award for 'warmest' congregation. At our main Sunday service each week, we have standing-room only, and our hugs are one of the reasons. I often warn those I invite that many of us are "Hug-a-holics." It's wonderful to see faces light up as arms reach out.

Hugs and Touch

(H)

What am I doing/willing to do to take care of my touch needs?

_____

_____

_____

_____

_____

_____

_____

_____

Listen to how often we use the phrases, "It was a touching moment" or "It just doesn't grab me." We are tactile creatures. Connecting with each other physically is one of the healthiest and most pleasurable of all our attitude adjustments.

Meanwhile, touch is not only fun for us; it's also good for those we touch. A friend of mine who speaks on wellness around the country tells her audiences, "If you don't hug your kids at home, you can be sure they'll get hugged in the back seat of a car." I find that even the teens who seem too cool for this kind of warmth still appreciate a tender touch.

▶ SAFE AND HEALTHY WAYS TO STAY IN TOUCH

So where do we begin? Here are some self-starters:

- Start small with co-workers or friends, perhaps with a pat on the arm, or clasping both hands during a handshake.

- Join a sports team or a dance group.

- Join a church, synagogue, temple or support group where they hug a lot.

- Hang around Italians or Spanish-speaking families.

- Offer your family members, from infants to adults, a daily backrub. To make it a game, use one of the wooden massage 'creatures' available at any bath and body store.

- Begin each meeting at work with staff members turning to their right and giving a backrub, then turning to their left and giving a 'thank-you' backrub. Make it optional, but make it fun!

We live in a cerebral society. Many of us live our lives through our heads. We think out every situation, but we do not feel them (with our hearts) or sense them (with our bodies). The good news is that once we learn to live in our skin, we won't be so 'absent-minded'; our minds will not be so absent from our physical bodies. We can use all our faculties to be more fully alive.

"Reach Out and Touch Someone" became a world-famous advertising slogan in the '80's, perhaps because it appealed to our hunger for physical connectedness. In a world of lawsuits and sexuality fears, E-mail and fax modems, cubicles and privacy fences, it is more important than ever to stay in touch.

See me, feel me, touch me, heal me.

From the Rock Opera *Tommy*

(H) Hugs and Touch

Insulate from the Negative

"Would you like a little cheese with your whining?"
Comment overheard at a restaurant

Anyone who has ever watched their weight knows that simply consuming more fruits and vegetables while downing daily malts, burgers and fries will not result in a healthy, trim body. So it is with our minds.

In order to be successful in our search for greater happiness, we must not only strengthen the positives in our lives, as we have covered so far. We must also become aware of bitter, blaming talk; hopeless and helpless song lyrics; and violent and belittling images on the television screen.

▶ INSIGHT OUT

But before we talk about what's outside of us, let's look back at what's inside of us. *All of life is our mirror.* Whatever we see around us is what is within us. That is why I can accept compliments so much more easily these days. Some compliments used to sadden me because it seemed like the sender was distancing himself or herself from me by placing me on a pedestal. Now I can calmly look a fan in the eye and say, "You wouldn't see it in me if it wasn't in you."

The same is true for the negative aspects we see in others. We can truly only 'see' what is in our Score range. We can see what is a little above our Score, or a little below, but not those things which are far beneath or beyond. Also, we only attract circumstances and individuals that are within our range. This means that when you first attract a job or a relationship, you are a 'like-attracts-like-match' for attitude and overall positive or negative focus.

In no way is this an excuse to stay in a relationship that doesn't feel good. When a dating or marriage relationship begins to involve destructive criticism, physical threats, days of pouting silence and/or dishonesty, you will feel it in the pit of your stomach. That is your stomach's way of saying you deserve better. Where does forgiveness enter in? You don't have to stay with abuse to forgive it.

▶ POSITIVE MINDSETTING

Now, let's refocus on some positive aspects. Take a deep breath and get into GA-GA (Gratitude and Appreciation). Think of the gifts you received in the "Every Day is Christmas" exercise which you completed in the chapter on Habit G. You have attracted all of those wonderful people and things because a lot of the time you are a grateful, loving and positive person. As you move into more consistent FGH mindsetting, you will attract more and more loving behavior from others, and your Score will skyrocket.

> *I keep the telephone of my mind open to peace,*
> *harmony, health, love, and abundance.*
> *Then whenever doubt, anxiety, or fear try to call me,*
> *they keep getting a busy signal,*
> *and soon they'll forget my number.*
>
> Edith Armstrong

▶ THE CHICKEN OR THE EGG-ON-YOUR-FACE?

So now, before heading into what we can do about *them*, let's remind ourselves that we *are* them. Or at least we *were* them until quite recently. Yes, I know, since reading this book you've done a complete turn-around (!?!), but you can still remember seeing life through their eyes, yes?

> *We have seen the enemy, and it is us.*
>
> Pogo

Okay, so now that we've refocused on "No Victims, Only Volunteers" thinking, it's obvious that the first thing we need to do when confronted with others' Non-Forgiving, Non-Grateful and Non-Hopeful words or actions is to take a deep breath and be grateful that we 'caught' it with our Awareness.

Secondly, we need to remember that what we give our focus (energy) to will grow. Therefore, fighting 'it', writing a letter to 'her' boss, or telling a horror story of what 'he' did to you at lunch today not only doesn't help, it hurts. It's not that you can never think about it, just don't dwell on it.

One analogy would be the difference between someone who is in a committed relationship noticing an attractive person or, on the other hand, flirting with them. The first is a look across the room. That is noticing them. But next, as you become conscious of your thoughts, you see yourself heading to a place in your mind where you don't really want to end up with your body. Therefore, you make a conscious choice to think of something else.

This turning your thoughts elsewhere doesn't have to be a panicked effort. A few seconds in a NON-FGH thought are not going to bring you major harm. In fact, to panic is to add one more negative factor to your thought process: *fear*. Rather, just non-judgmentally notice and go from there.

"But what if I don't refocus? What if I stay in judgment of someone, fear of something, or lust over someone who's not available?" No problem, really. Just prepare yourself to get what you focus on. You will attract more judgment, the very thing you fear, or betrayal on some level...until you refocus on what you *really* want.

▶ INSULATING FROM THE NEGATIVE IS AN INSIDE JOB

Group sports are fun, but one thing I love about golf, or other individual sports like track or swimming, is that what others do really makes no difference to the final outcome. If I get my score low enough in any of these three arenas, I will win. Other people 'not doing their part' does not affect me. That is how it is with our thoughts.

We are much more naturally insulated than we believe. No one arguing with us or putting us down can affect our Score *unless we make a choice to let them.* I can even use a moment of their negativity to skyrocket my Score as I focus on my greater than ever desire to return to FGH and the Joy that it brings.

So, now that we've covered the most important part of the insulation, let's move to the secondary level: insulating ourselves from undue negativity around us.

▶ GOOD, BETTER, BEST

Insulating ourselves from the negativity of others doesn't mean we can't *spend time with them.* We don't even need to try and change them. It's not that their choice is *all* bad, it's just not always as good as we would like for ourselves.

To return to the junk food analogy, there is nothing inherently wrong with hamburgers, french fries, or malts. Even though they are not the best for us, they are not inherently bad. Stephen Covey, in a recent lecture series stated, "The worst enemy of the best is not the bad. It is the good." He was pointing out that a Good vs. Bad decision is easy to make. It is when we must choose between good and better that the difficulty arises.

We can feed junk food to our brains just as we can feed it to our bodies; however, there will be a price to pay. In the past, we were unaware of the effects of words, images, and actions, just as previous generations were unaware of the negative effects of asbestos. But we can no longer claim naiveté. We now have a choice whether or not we want to heighten our awareness of those elements that may affect us negatively.

▶ AWARENESS OF THE BIG PICTURE

We sometimes become so inundated by the fog of negatives surrounding us that we don't realize that the air is clearer elsewhere. Tina Turner's former abusive husband once remarked, "I don't hit her any harder than my Daddy hit my Momma!"

I believe we become what we think, what we hear, what we see, what we say, and whom we associate with. The few times I have gone with friends to a casino, for example, the ratio of smokers is usually greater than 50% of the patrons, but I feel more in danger from second-hand despair than second-hand smoke. There is nothing wrong with casinos in and of themselves, but I do not believe that they are in my best interest.

Similarly, I have heard employees make such remarks as, "Of course we have to work seven days a week. Everybody does it if they want to get ahead." Many people limit their vision of what is possible to the individuals in their immediate circle of friends and co-workers. In this case, it becomes even more important to have friends and co-workers who challenge us to live healthier, happier lives.

> *Tell me thy company, and I'll tell thee what thou art.*
> From Cervantes' *Don Quixote*

Once we become *Aware* of our choices, we can move to *Acceptance* of our responsibility to search out the best option. We then must choose *Accurate Assessments* in order to face the fears that inevitably accompany initiating change. Finally, we can take an *Action* to move toward the best life offers.

▶ DERAILING NEGATIVITY AND JUDGMENTS

"But how? When there are so many negative people around me?" The most important thing to remember when we are around negativity is that it is only contagious if we allow it to be. When we encounter something that makes us feel uncomfortable, unhappy or upset, we can simply see it as contrasting with where we want to be: a kind of trampoline off which to bounce.

Thanks to this experience, we get clearer about what we don't want, and that brings us clarity on what we do want. We can actually become grateful for the circumstance or individual causing our discomfort. When they go off on their negative path, we can just say, "Wow, that's an interesting way to think. Thank you for sharing," and then go about our day.

▶ BOUNDARIES FOR A BETTER LIFE

There are many times in a normal week when a negative message of fear or hopelessness is telegraphed to our unsuspecting brains. We can stay alert to catch these messages and choose not to buy into them. Here are some of the steps I have taken recently to protect my attitude, my energy and my health and well being.

- **Billboards and Advertising:** If I read a negative message, I protect myself from the fall-out by stating an affirmation. A billboard for Miller Lite had the slogan "Catch a Cold" right next to a beer can. A billboard for an emergency care center read, "Tis the Season to be Sneezin'." When I see these, I remind myself how healthy I am and how grateful I am for my healthy body.

- **Self-Talk:** Author Louise Hay claims that our subconscious hears every negative statement as though it were about ourselves. If I overhear an individual who is using negative self-talk, I may simply move to another area, or say something like, "Excuse me, did you hear what you just said?"

  When a newly hired secretary wrote herself a note which read, "Push the hold button, stupid!" and taped it to the phone, I asked her to remove it and encouraged her to take my class. Instead she resigned, which worked out fine too.

- **Movies:** Not too long ago, members of my women's group and I walked out midway through a movie. We weren't thrilled with a lot of the early scenes, but when the mother of a character dismissed her daughter's resistance to dating a married man with, "You're too picky," we left.

  Another time a friend and I attended the premier of "The Patriot." I noticed that I was the only one to walk out of the theater of this extremely violent film. When I ask people why they stay watching films that take them to such not-feeling-good places, they often tell me they want to "get their money's worth." I believe some money is too expensive.

- **Music:** My kids and I were visiting a friend at her cabin one afternoon when rap music began blaring next door. When a CD full of songs using profanity came on, I suggested that the kids and I go run an errand. Instead, my friend went over and asked the neighbors to change the CD, which they quickly did, apologizing that they hadn't noticed what was playing. Their subconscious noticed. We can become conscious anytime.

  I am equally aware of the helpless messages in many of today's love songs. "I can't live without you" songs, for example, encourage co-dependent thinking. I don't want that message. If I couldn't live without him, I'd have been dead long ago!

- **Magazines:** I remember seeing one publication in a physician's waiting room whose name I did not recognize. The cover read, "The Truth About the Economy." The articles inside this monthly publication described everything from dark and terrible 'plots' by the IRS to global bank frauds. I asked the doctor why she had such a magazine in her office area. She said she was unaware of it.

When we take a closer look at what we see and listen more carefully to what we hear, we realize what messages we have been sending to our brains. Awareness then motivates us to make changes.

Observe for one week the messages around you. If you can, notice without going into anger. Simply be grateful for the awareness and refocus your thoughts elsewhere.

What I've observed this week:

_____

_____

_____

_____

_____

_____

_____

_____

_____

_____

_____

▶ ONCE UPON A TELEVISION

Easily my greatest concern regarding negativity affecting our families and ourselves is with television. Because we have been slow to admit the effects of TV on our thinking and behaviors, its effects are all the greater.

Today, families spend a higher percentage of waking time in front of the TV than in any other activity. Before the average child of today graduates from high school, he or she will have spent 15,000 hours watching television, compared to 11,000 hours in school. How does this affect us? Insidiously.

These are some incidents in my own life which are telling evidence of the seductive power of television:

- A few years ago, I was invited to a family dinner where the head of the table was occupied by a television set. Our entire meal was dominated by the 'special' show.

- My friend's 3 year-old said she wanted a certain doll for Christmas, "batteries not included." By the time she was four, this little girl knew the line-up of shows for every night of the week.

- Not long ago I helped with a ninth-grade retreat at a Catholic high school. One of the girls in my small group prayed for "Jimmy, who died yesterday." Her girlfriend snickered and said, "The actor didn't die, just the character." We were praying for a soap opera character!

> *All television is educational television.*
> *The question is, what is it teaching?*
>
> Nicholas Johnson

Because we are in a relaxed, alpha brain-wave state when we watch TV, we are even more receptive to its messages. One reason why so many people feel helpless about issues such as violence is because they watch and buy into an unrealistic representation of the problem. For example, police on TV use their guns 10 times more than in real life. By the age of 18, TV viewers have seen over 12,000 graphic murders and assaults. When we feel overwhelmed and helpless, we are prone to give up.

▶ THE FEAR FACTOR

In a CBS *Frontline* program hosted by Bill Moyers in 1995, the claim was made that a child who watches a lot of TV (over 2 hours a day) begins to believe in a meaner world. "They are more afraid because they feel so vulnerable. TV creates a great amount of fear," according to their research. This fear does not only affect children. Adults who watch more than two hours a day of TV are not only more prone to violence, they are less hopeful, more prejudicial, and more fearful.

> *Television is an invention that permits you to*
> *be entertained in your living room*
> *by people you wouldn't have in your home.*
>
> David Frost

A prime example of the power of television to promote fear in children was brought to my attention after the '95 Oklahoma City Federal Building bombing. A week after the incident, a good friend of mine received a call from the Red Cross inviting her to volunteer for a special two-day counseling hotline set up in South Dakota. When I asked her why she was going to South Dakota to counsel children from Oklahoma, she corrected me. "We're counseling children from other states around the country who were traumatized by the disaster."

I reflected on the moods of my 4 and 11-year-old children that particular week. "My kids weren't traumatized," I offered for discussion.

"That's because they don't come home and turn on the television like most kids do. Thousands of children watched the replays of the disaster half a dozen times before their parents even got home."

When discussing television with parents, I often hear, "What do you expect me to do?" The real question is, "What do you want to do?" We can feel like victims of our own technology, afraid to pull the plug on what we have created, or we can remind ourselves of the spectrum of possibilities for taming the television tiger.

> *A small group of committed citizens can change the world.*
> *Indeed, it is the only thing that ever has.*
>
> Margaret Mead

▶ RECLAIMING OUR POWER

In his book, *Six Points For Raising Happy, Healthy Children,* syndicated columnist John Rosemond states, "I don't believe there's any justification for letting a preschool child watch any television at all." Based on years of research into the deficiencies in the competency skills of TV-viewing children, he recommends a limited number of quality programs to be viewed only once the child learns to read.

I know many families who choose not to own a television. Still others limit the number of hours the TV is on each day. Another group of families choose to move the television out of the main family room into a room such as an unfinished basement, only bringing it upstairs for special shows.

Still other families shut off the TV around holy days or during the summer. This hiatus gives them a new sense of objectivity toward the programs that they sometimes believe they 'can't live without'. The year we turned off our TV for the forty days of Lent, it took us about a week to 'forget' about the tube. We didn't miss it for the rest of the season.

> *"No way! What would I do?"*
> *– a 10 year old's answer to the Frontline question,*
> *"If we gave you a million dollars never to watch TV again,*
> *would you take it?"*

What is the maximum amount of time you want to view TV each week?

_____

What is the maximum amount of time you want your children to view TV each week?

_____

What changes will you make to achieve your goal? (e.g., move the TV to a less accessible room)

_____

_____

_____

_____

_____

_____

_____

_____

_____

_____

Re-read the 101 risks on page 40. Then, as a family, select two or three each month to work into your lifestyle!

Re-read the 101 risks on page 40.

▶ NEGATIVITY IN THE WORKPLACE

Beyond television, there are other forms of negativity to be aware of. One I'm frequently asked about is the co-worker who only has 'awful' stories to tell each day at work, or who sees every situation as hopeless.

What can we do? Consider what an asthmatic would do around a smoker:

- Ask the 'fuming' person to fume elsewhere,
- Move until they're done fuming, or
- Move/change jobs or departments.

There is an addiction to blame.
Each third party who sides with me about my grievances
gives me a "fix" that keeps me going.

Dr. Mary Riley

▶ POSITIVES ON DECK

One innovative high school teacher put a simple sign on the new deck outside his house: the word "negative" with a circle around it and a red line through it. This "No Negative" warning was so highly respected that a young married couple rang his doorbell at ten o'clock one night to ask to spend time on the protected deck.

The faster we want our lives to change for the better, the more diligent we will become in surrounding ourselves with the best. Five minutes of affirmation will not negate hours of fear-based discussion at work. The negative aspects promoting fear and despair must be balanced by an even greater positive focus on love, courage, gratitude and hope.

None of the activities mentioned in this section are inherently bad or evil. Therefore, in confronting them, there is no need to harbor resentments if our requests for change are not granted. To do so would create more negativity.

On the contrary, it does not benefit us to make eradication of negativity our primary life focus, because we create more of what we focus on. As the former creative director of Hallmark, Gordon MacKenzie, shared at a seminar I attended:

Only the novice motorcyclist focuses on the danger of the car backing out of the driveway. That is why he has so many accidents. The veteran will keep his eyes on the goal ahead, thereby maneuvering safely around the potential danger.

Mother Teresa was once asked to take part in a march against hunger. She responded that she would never march *against* anything, but that if they ever organized a march *for* something, they should contact her again.

We can spend our time organizing pickets against television, newspapers, magazines, movies, rap music, destructive criticism or casinos. But to create the life we want for ourselves, it is better to simply 'pick-it'. Once we move in a more positive direction, our environment will begin to transform itself. Thus, insulating from the negative will be less of a challenge, and inviting the positive will be **an easier** choice.

Don't fight war. Create peace.

Marianne Williamson

Journal

*Journaling allows more
of the totality of what we are to come alive.*

G.F Simmons

Journaling. Power writing. Keeping a diary. Whatever it's called, a few minutes each day to let your inner voice speak on paper can literally transform your life. It is as simple as getting out a paper and pen. There are no rules about what to write, how long to write, or what to do with the writings when you are finished.

Why journal? It relaxes us. It 'halves the griefs and doubles the joys' of life when we get what is inside of us outside of us. Most importantly, it reveals the hidden agendas that keep us from greater fulfillment and joy.

The wisdom we connect with when we go within has been called by many names: The wise old woman or man within, Sophia, the Holy Spirit, Universal Consciousness, All That Is, Oneness. In her wonderful book, *The Artist's Way,* author Julia Cameron suggests that G.O.D. can refer to Good Orderly Direction. It doesn't matter what we call this Source. We just have to trust it is there, at all times, with creativity and happiness as its calling card.

*Silence is as full of potential wisdom
as the unhewn marble of great sculpture.*

Aldous Huxley

So why don't we all rush to get out pens and pads each day? Because we know that our inner wisdom exacts a high price for joy: gut-level honesty. We must face our hidden agendas. One gentleman had the courage to admit he needed more courage. "I am becoming aware that I'm not ready to become aware," he shared with the group. While admiring his honesty, we reminded him there is no way to get to the castle without first going through the dark forest.

▶ THE KEY TO OUR BASEMENT

When we do not take the time to process the intense emotions of our experiences, we have to 'store' some of the left-overs in our 'basement'. This is the subconscious, which most psychologists believe runs our lives. We truly "know not what we do."

This is why mental health experts agree that less than 10% of achieving behavioral change is due to will power. Over 75% of our transformation is by getting to the core subconscious issues. Samuel Taylor Coleridge once wrote that no one does anything from a single motive. Journaling gets to the problem behind the problem in our basement and brings it to light. Once we know the real issue, the solution is much clearer and close at hand.

Journal

J ▶ THE BUSTER BREAKTHROUGH

The power of journaling was made clear to me on a gray fall day years ago. I was driving home from the store when I saw our 5-month-old kitten Buster lying in the street. He had been hit by a car and killed. When I broke the news to my then 6-year-old daughter, we cried and hugged for quite awhile, finally deciding to bury Buster in the back yard.

Three weeks later, I came across one of Buster's toys under the couch. I sat down and wept uncontrollably. As I wept, I realized that my daughter had, by all appearances, completed her grief process. The day after Buster's death, we had bought the bird she requested, which was now the beloved family pet. Why was I still so broken up over this kitten that had lived with us for only a few months? I decided to journal.

I got out a sheet of paper and began to write, "The good thing about crying so hard about Caramel's death is..." I wrote no further, as I had my answer.

Caramel had been *my* kitten that was run over when I was six. The day of the accident my well-meaning parents had told me not to cry, for fear of upsetting the younger children or increasing the sadness of my uncle who had been behind the wheel of the car. Had I not journaled, I might not have become aware of the need for healing this powerful childhood memory.

Journaling can write your childhood wrongs.

Catherine L. Taylor

Often, as we begin to journal, our subconscious takes over, revealing insights that can help us make decisions, calm our fears, or make more sense of our past. Once we turn off our TV channels, the channel that goes 24 hours a day within us has many secrets to reveal.

Journal about journaling.

1. What have I noticed about my reaction to the journaling exercises offered in this workbook?

_____

_____

_____

_____

_____

_____

_____

_____

2. What are my real thoughts, feelings, and concerns, around this form of confidential writing?

_____

_____

_____

_____

_____

_____

_____

_____

▶ How to Begin

As with any habit, it is helpful to prepare mentally and physically for journaling. You may want to make a commitment with a friend that each of you will write for five minutes a day for one week, and share your general insights at the end of the week. Or you may want to go out and buy a blank book in which to keep your writings. Preparation of any kind increases the likelihood of your following through with your goal.

To begin, I always date my entries, even if I am writing on a napkin that I plan to throw away as soon as I leave the restaurant. This step calls me to 'be here now' and gets me started with the writing. The first words always seem the most challenging to get onto paper.

Beyond that, I don't suggest any one technique for journaling. Just see what comes out. One woman shared that the previous night she journaled just one word, "Damn!"

A gentleman shared that one evening he wrote down, "I do _not_ want to journal tonight," then continued to write for four very illuminating pages! When he asked me why such a thing had occurred, I offered that his honesty was a means of connecting powerfully with his Inner Wisdom.

When I journal, I can:

1.   Write in poetry or pig-Latin,

2.   Doodle for days or dangle my participles,

3.   Write with my non-dominant hand about my non-dominant spouse,

4.   Write a letter to myself, to God, to my boss, or to a deceased relative.

Journaling is simple, but once again, not always easy.

Get out of the way...
Accumulate pages, not judgments...
Leap, and the net will appear.

Julia Cameron

▶ BARRIERS TO JOURNALING

As simple as the process of journaling is, most of us still balk at the thought of it and rush to our excuses:

1. **"I'm afraid I'll do it wrong!"**

    Despite my objections, one woman in my class was adamant that she had "done it wrong." Upon further inquiry, she admitted she had written with a pencil and erased. Her classmates encouraged her to find a safe hiding place for her writings and change from pencil to pen.

    When you are finished, if you still have qualms about your papers ending up in the wrong hands, you might use a burning ritual while you express your gratitude for the wisdom and freedom of the journaling experience.

2. **"I can't find the time."**

    No one has ever 'found' 5–10 minutes a day. Time must be set aside. Stephen Covey points out that if we do not make time for what is *important* but not *urgent* (journaling, rest, relationships, exercise, etc.), we will find our lives consumed by what is *important* and *urgent* (illness, arguments, accidents, crises.)

3. **"It would be like Pandora's box. Too much would come out!"**

    This reference to the Greek myth of the woman who opened a forbidden box, only to turn loose the demons of the world, reminds me of a recent divorcee in one of my classes. "I think I'd kill him if I journaled!" she argued. I suggested that her chances of killing him were much greater if she did not journal.

    I recall a speaker who came to my high school classroom to talk about drugs.

    He agreed that the subconscious 'basement' stores the overflow of joys, anxieties, and sorrows. He added that the psyche 'brings up' things from our basement slowly, never giving us more than we can handle... unless we are on a drug like LSD. "Then the drug rips a hole in the psyche and we get inordinate amounts of joy or pain." If we are not on LSD, our psyche will be our guardian from overwhelming pain.

1. Select one of the following 10 Journaling Ideas.

2. Write out 2–3 sentences about how you feel before beginning.

_____

_____

_____

3. Complete the exercise.

4. After you finish write out 2–3 sentences about the process.

_____

_____

_____

_____

_____

_____

10 Journaling Ideas — select one of the following:

1 Complete the phrase, " I am becoming aware..." 10–15 times.

_____

_____

_____

_____

_____

_____

_____

_____

_____

_____

_____

Journal **J**

2 Make a gratitude list of at least 10 items, five of them from the past 24 hours.

_____

_____

_____

_____

_____

_____

_____

_____

_____

3 Write 2 endings for each of the following phrases:

"I am…"

"I realize…"

"I want…"

"I will…"

"I know…

_____

_____

_____

_____

_____

_____

_____

_____

_____

4 Take five minutes to complete the phrase, "If I were willing to see what I see and know what I know…" on a separate sheet of paper 6–10 times.

5 Write yourself a love letter on a separate sheet of paper. Whatever you would most like to hear from your real or imagined partner, say it. Make it as long as the letter you would most like to receive.

6 Ask your body to speak to you. What is your back telling you? Your head? What are you feet telling you? Your eyes? Your hands? Your stomach?

_____

_____

_____

_____

_____

_____

_____

_____

7 Remember back to the last few compliments you have received. Write them down word for word. Now really let each of them sink in. How would you feel if you met you on the street tomorrow? Would these qualities attract you?

_____

_____

_____

_____

_____

_____

_____

_____

8 Write, on a separate sheet of paper, the eulogy that you would like read at your funeral.

9 Write on truth. What is the most challenging thing for you to write about right now? When are you most truthful? Have any experiences in life taught you that honesty is sometimes too painful? What feelings or actions are the most difficult for you to accept? To write about? To admit to others?

_____

_____

_____

_____

_____

_____

_____

_____

_____

_____

_____

_____

10 Visualize tomorrow going really well. Now pretend it is the day after tomorrow. Write down your description of your wonderful yesterday in detail, looking back on what a great experience it was!

_____

_____

_____

_____

_____

_____

_____

_____

_____

_____

_____

► OUR SECRETS KEEP US SICK

I recall most vividly how journaling opened up a closed heart in a man I thought would never budge. It all began in the training headquarters of a large plant.

"This is a reminder that you may drop this class after the introductory session if you are not comfortable with the personal nature of Mary Kay's material. However, let us remind you of the excellent ratings she is getting from all levels of our employees...."

Mike sat in the very back row, strong arms crossed tightly in front of his chest, listening hard. Nobody was gonna call him a quitter! Then it was my turn.

"The real instructor for this course is sitting in your chair. I will stir some things up inside of you, but the best insights will come from a process called 'journaling'. I want to encourage you to take just five minutes of quiet writing time each day during this 4-week course..." Mike mulled it over. Nobody was gonna say he didn't do the homework!

Much later I learned what Mike had written those first few weeks. He shared that the first week was primarily about how much he hated journaling! The second week he moved to how much he hated the class! The third week his focus became how much he hated *me*! Then, about 21 days into the process, something snapped. Even Mike got tired of hearing Mike complain.

That night, as he sat down to write in his spiral notebook, Mike wrote for five minutes about Viet Nam. The tears flowed as his pen poured out his pain. He was very grateful when the five minutes were up. The next day, Mike spoke up in class. It wasn't a lot, but some of us noticed that his arms weren't crossed any more.

The class ended with an announcement that due to the popularity of the program, we were now going to offer a kind of graduate course for this material. Mike was the first one to sign up. I was stunned.

As the second course drew to a close, I knew I would miss the gentle humor of this sweet man who had opened up about his hopes and dreams, his pain and healing. At the final class, as we were sharing hugs around the room, he slipped me two thank-you notes. One was from Mike. The other was from his wife. It is hers I will never forget.

> "Dear *Mary Kay,*
>
> *How can I ever thank you for the changes I have seen in Mike? Before coming to your classes, his average number of hours per week at the plant was 70 or more. Last week he only worked 45 hours, and Sunday we went for our first walk in over 20 years. He has found such peace. God Bless you and the wonderful work that you do."*

When the student is ready the teacher will appear.
When the teacher is ready the student will appear.

What is my Score these days?

_____

Am I willing to make a commitment to myself at this time to journal daily?

_____

If so, for how many days and for how long each day?

_____

If not, write an acceptance statement of your decision to focus on other tools for now.

_____

_____

_____

_____

_____

_____

When we are unable to find tranquility within ourselves,
it is useless to seek it elsewhere.

François de La Rochefoucauld

Journaling is house-cleaning. It differs from thinking about something, which just rearranges the heirlooms and junk in our attics. Writing out our thoughts and feelings is the equivalent of giving a whole bunch of stuff to the Salvation Army. It gets our feelings out of our gut and onto paper.

There are many ways to house-clean our inner selves: a therapy session, a walk with a close friend, a drunken stupor, a nervous breakdown. However, journaling is the easiest and most accessible tool with which to do the work of consciousness on a regular basis.

If you bring forth what is within you,
what you bring forth will save you.
If you do not bring forth what is within you,
what you do not bring forth will destroy you.

The Gospel of Thomas

Keep On Keeping On

The only thing that stands between you and grand
success in living are these two things:
getting started and never quitting!
Dr. Robert Schuller

We are an instant society. We like fast food, fast cars, and fast cures. We have surgery rather than change our life style. We get a divorce rather than see a counselor. We do faxes, E-mails, and World Wide Web for instant access.

Perhaps the most alarming component of our instant-society is that we are betting more and more every year in hopes of becoming 'Instant Winners'. The truth is there is no such thing. All winning takes time. All winners are patient.

Most people give up just when they're about to achieve success.
They quit on the one-yard line.
They give up at the last minute of the game,
one foot from a winning touchdown.
Ross Perot

Learning takes time. Loving takes time. Living to the full takes time. How have we forgotten these important life truths? More importantly, how can we remember them?

Perhaps the simplest way to remind ourselves and our children of the value of patience is to start a garden. When my son grew his first plant in a plastic cup, he would check it every day for progress. The only thing that kept him from spooning that dirt into his piles in the backyard was our daily assurance that a sprout would emerge. When the grass grew, it was sacred to him, his very own 'miracle'. His next planting project was not nearly so challenging.

Faith is a seed, in ourselves, in a program, or in a higher power, and it is one of the most important ingredients for a healthy and happy life. Once we have faith, we will have patience. Once we have patience, we will have success.

Nothing in the world can take the place of persistence.
Talent will not... Genius will not... Education alone will not.
Persistence and determination alone are omnipotent.
Calvin Coolidge

The other lesson a garden teaches us, besides faith, is faithfulness. A garden begun and then left untended can overwhelm a plot of land, resulting not only in low yield, but a high workload at the end of summer. Once we see the first fruits of our labors, we cannot stop working the garden, or the program that brought them forth.

Keep On Keeping On

> *Be like a postage stamp — stick to one thing until you get there.*
>
> Josh Billings

I am often asked if I faithfully practice exercise, journaling, and affirmations every day. I have done each of these daily for a year or two at different times in my life. Now, I can say that I do at least one of the above every day. I vary them with my needs, desires, and schedule. The other skills I use every day — hugging, prayer and meditation, optimistic thinking, asking for what I want, monitoring self-talk, limiting media, showing gratitude, singing, smiling and reading motivational literature — have surely changed my life for the better.

Each individual's personal program will be worked in his or her own unique way. But it must be worked regularly to yield long-lasting results. Too discouraging? We have all been brushing our teeth daily for years, and the only real feedback has been a good report on our annual trip to the dentist. Your level of success depends on your level of commitment.

So how do we learn patience and persistence? By facing the three greatest enemies of Keep On Keeping on: boredom, discomfort, and surviving the rocks.

▶ THE THREE GREATEST ENEMIES OF KEEP ON KEEPING ON

> *This thing we call "failure" is not*
> *falling down, but staying down.*
>
> Mary Pickford

▶ Enemy #1: Boredom

I had the opportunity to interview a four-time NCAA champion wrestler not long ago. When I asked him to tell me about the hard times he spoke of boredom. "My dad and my coach were always on me to practice the fundamentals, when I wanted to practice the more exciting stuff... Their coaching won me the championships. On the days when I was really tense or so tired I couldn't see straight, my body still remembered the fundamentals from all those drills."

Finding our motivation from the excitement of the long-term goal, rather than from the excitement of the moment, results in the pay-off of persistence. We can use our imagination to feel the feelings of our eventual success as easily as we can recall the feelings of our last disappointment. By using our imagination to play over and over the possible 'success scenarios', boredom won't have a chance.

> *Big shots are only little shots who keep shooting.*
>
> Christopher Morley

▶ Enemy #2: Discomfort

In her audiotape *Why People Don't Heal*, Caroline Myss displays a disdain for those of us who whine whenever we feel uncomfortable.

"You must take the program in your mind and drop it to your will and shove it down there and say, 'This is what you will do. You will get up in the morning and exercise everyday for any hour. I don't care how you feel, you will do it.' You begin to take these things your mind knows and force yourself to live them, no matter how uncomfortable you are. When you get stuck, say to yourself, 'Comfort is not my business; healing is.' It is irrelevant that you are tired, uncomfortable, and exhausted. Who cares?"

The challenge flies the face of modern day conveniences. As I write this, a friend of mine is on his annual fishing trip. He and his group will get up very early tomorrow morning, climb into a boat, and hope for hungry fish. In their Canadian surroundings "the call of the wild" will excite their all-male crew with the smells of adventure. Then, just a few hours into their outing, other smells will excite them. The host will drive up in a small boat, bringing fresh fruit, rolls and coffee. Roughing it nowadays means no room service!

▶ Enemy #3: Surviving The Rocks

A few years back, my fifth grade daughter did her school hero report on Wilma Rudolph. From her research, she learned that Wilma had to fight tremendous odds to achieve success. She was born premature, the twentieth of 22 children. She was raised in severe poverty and had to deal with the racism of the '40's and '50's. She also came down with polio, making it impossible for her to walk without braces until the age of eleven.

Wilma credits her mother's wisdom as the key to her ability to overcome obstacles and sustain a positive attitude. "My mother taught me very early to believe I could achieve any accomplishment I wanted to." Fueled by great persistence, as well as a dream of a better life, Wilma became the first woman ever to win three gold medals in track at the 1960 Olympics.

Wilma Rudolph's overcomer story is similar to so many: Charles Barkley in basketball, Colonel Sanders in the restaurant business and Abraham Lincoln in politics, to name just a few. The message for us, and for our children, is that every challenge in life can make us better or bitter.

When you get into a tight place and everything goes against you,
and it seems as though you could not hang on a minute longer;
never give up then, for that is just the place and time
that the tide will turn.

Harriet Beecher Stowe

▶ THE DREAMS THAT WOULD NOT DIE

Of all the overcomer stories I have read (over 1000), one of the most vivid for me is the story of Gary Willie. Gary was a young black teen in the '60's who had no money for college. His only hope was the recruiter who came to his high school each spring to choose one or two young men for an athletic scholarship.

The day of the try-outs, Gary gave his all but was not selected for the honor. His best friend was chosen instead. The summer day he waved good-bye as his friend left for college on the bus, Gary ran to his coach's office, sobbing. "I've got to go, Coach. All I've ever dreamed of was going to college."

"How much money do you have, Willie?" asked the coach.

"About twenty dollars."

"That's enough for a one-way bus fare. Take your money and go to your college."

Gary did just that. He hid out in his friend's dorm room, eating food his friend snuck out of the cafeteria. Every day he would show up at practice and go through the drills on the sideline. Everyday he would ask the coach for another chance, and every day he was told to go back home.

Near the end of the summer, Gary decided to try one more thing. He had his friend sneak him into the locker room, where he hid in an empty locker. When everyone had gone home that night, he climbed out and scrubbed the entire area until it shone.

When the coach walked in the next morning, he smiled, heaved a sigh, and told Gary to come into his office. There he said he would personally pay the student's $10 registration fee and offered him a scholarship, but only for one year.

One year become four and Gary Willie got his degree. So, how did I hear about him? I read a one-page article in *People* magazine. Gary Willie, attorney-at law, had just donated $10 million dollars to Shaw University, the largest individual donation to an alma mater to date.

Progress, not perfection.

The AA Big Book

▶ THE POWER OF PERSISTANCE

Recently I came across another perfect example of keeping your eye on the goal and not letting anything deter you.

A.C. Lyles has worked for Paramount Pictures since he was 14. At the age of 82 his office is in the same building where Adolph Zukor built Paramount into one of the greatest film studios of all time during the '20's and '30's. As a child, Lyles met Zukor while working at a movie theatre in Jacksonville, Florida. He told the studio head that he wanted a job with Paramount in Hollywood and Zukor told him "to stay in touch."

Lyles responded by writing Zukor every Sunday for a year and a half. Then Zukor's secretary sent a note that a couple of letters a year would be fine. Lyles, not one to miss an opportunity, began writing to both Zukor and his secretary every week. When Gary Cooper made a visit to the Florida theatre where Lyles worked, the teenager talked the famous actor into scribbling a note to Zukor to the effect that Lyles was deserving of a Paramount job.

Facing such determination, Zukor hired the 18 year old Lyles after he graduated from high school and arrived in California in 1937 with $48, two jars of peanut butter and two loaves of bread. Zukor quickly put him in the publicity department and the two remained friends until Zukor's death at the age of 103.

Lyles became well known among the great stars and directors of Hollywood, eventually delivering eulogies for such greats as his friend Gary Cooper.

Commitment to friendship, a cause, a community, or a course of action can only come with the knowledge that every step makes a difference to the final outcome.

Not long ago, a 48-year-old counselor was having lunch with her hair stylist when the former revealed why she was no longer counseling. "I'm pregnant... with twins!" It was her first pregnancy, but her third marriage. "Every painful lesson I have learned until now has been worth it," she shared with her friend. "Now that I know how happy I can be, I wouldn't ~~~~ ~~~~e thing leading up to this moment."

Ask yourself:

Would I have written off a counselor who had two "failed" marriages?

_____

When and why do I tend to give up on people?

_____
_____
_____
_____
_____

When and why do I tend to give up on myself?

_____
_____
_____
_____
_____

How many positive events need to happen before I trust someone or something?

_____

How many negative events need to happen before I stop trusting?

_____

► WAIT-POWER

Working the program described in this book does not require much will power. It is more about patience and persistence, what I call 'wait-power' as we change the way we think about ourselves, others, and life.

Fall seven times, stand up eight.
Japanese Proverb

Have you noticed how many quotes there are in this section? I could list quotes of thousands of men and women who have been recognized for their great achievements because most of them have, at one time or another, spoken of or written on the importance of persistence. Of all the threads that connect writings on changing your life and improving your attitude, perseverance reigns as the strongest determinant.

In the game of life,
nothing is less important than the score at half time.
Anonymous

Whether it be for a gold medal or for a golden opportunity, each dream is achieved one step at a time. And no steps are ever in vain. Each stumbling block can turn into a stepping stone along the path of life. I recently overheard a silver-haired artist sharing with an admirer about her works. When the younger person asked the painter how long it took her to complete the portrait before them, her answer was, "72 years."

You have set yourselves a difficult task,
but you will succeed if you persevere;
and you will find a joy in overcoming obstacles.
Remember, no effort that we make to attain something beautiful is ever lost.
Helen Keller

Lighten Up and Laugh ☺! Ⓛ

*You grow up the day you have the first real laugh —
at yourself.*

Ethel Barrymore

We don't need a magnifying glass to see the humor-happiness connection. Come on, face it. You opened this section hoping for a couple of good jokes. Okay, okay...but before I give you my favorites, I want you to figure out yours.

Think back to three or four of the funniest incidents in your life or the lives of those you know. Write down some key words, like:

• Driving through a car wash with the sun roof open.

• Laughing so hard I fell out of the boat.

_____

_____

_____

_____

_____

_____

Now, think back to the three or four funniest jokes or stories you've ever heard. Write down key phrases for these as well:

_____

_____

_____

_____

_____

_____

_____

▶ HUMOR AND OUR IQ

In the 1980's, Professor Howard Gardner's research concluded that there were actually seven areas of IQ: math, verbal, kinesthetic, musical, spatial, intrapersonal and interpersonal. His work has sparked amazing insights into the variety of combinations of gifts in the human community. Recent studies now indicate that there is an eighth area as well: a sense of humor IQ.

Because my main gift is intrapersonal, this book is about understanding ourselves. But we all have at least a small gift in each of the areas. Just as we want to exercise math and verbal areas of the brain to keep them in shape, so it is important to keep our sense of humor toned up as well.

> *A waist is a terrible thing to mind.*
>
> Refrigerator magnet

Since the sense of humor is not one of my naturally strong areas, I have to work at it. That is, if you can call it work to listen to Stephen Wright and watch the video *Airplane* annually! I also use cartoons, comedy shows, refrigerator magnets, humorous e-mails and my girlfriends as humor stimulants from time to time.

With the completion of the first exercise in this section, you now have a "funny file."

I keep mine handy for whenever the mood hits. Just as I often have cravings for Mexican food, sometimes I just have to rent a Jerry Seinfeld or Robin Williams video. Just as I may go to a movie to help me cry, I may also go to a comedy club to help me laugh.

Laughing and crying are actually extremely closely connected. Look back to your list of funniest real-life occurrences from the above exercise. In every instance, the person involved could have laughed or cried. The difference between the two is simply one of distance.

In the early '90's, singer-songwriter Bette Midler crooned, "From a distance, the world looks blue and green..." The song goes on to say to how much calmer and more peaceful things would seem if we would look at them from afar. Laughter is 'getting some distance' on an incident we might be tempted to take too personally.

The true personal life incidents I'll be sharing with you in the upcoming pages were all potentially mortifying experiences. Thank heavens laughter helped us all survive them.

> *I know that tragedy + time = humor.*
> *But I say, why wait?*
>
> T. Marni Vos

▶ INCISION DERISION

A friend of mine I'll call Billy, (so he'll stay a friend of mine), had an embarrassing moment during his senior year in high school. The teacher at his parochial school was covering various religious rites with her seniors.

On this particular Friday, she asked a hypothetical question, "You all know what circumcision is, don't you?" Immediately, Billy's hand flew up in the air. Since Billy didn't speak up all that often, the teacher was curious about what he wanted to add to the discussion. "Yes, Billy?" she asked.

"It's when they cut the skin off your forehead," Billy offered. According to my sources, I am told that was the last comment he made in class his senior year.

▶ WHAT'S ALL THE HOOP-LA?

At a party for our pastor's anniversary, we had a hula-hoop contest for all ages. It was simple: if you kept the hoop going longer than anyone else in your group, you made it to the finals.

Being an athlete and a bit of a perfectionist, a dear friend of mine went into her round with gusto and determination; so much so that when they played the music for her to begin, she "hula-ed" the hoop right over her head. You could say she really hooped it up! (Very punny!) I laughed so hard I could barely breathe.

▶ CAUGHT AT THE CHRISTMAS CRIB

The week before Christmas things are always bustling around our house. The year my daughter Joanna was ten we put the Nativity crib out in our sunroom, a room she played in often. One evening that week I was in the dining room wrapping packages when I heard her exclaim from the sunroom, "Jesus!"

Hardly able to believe I had heard such profanity from my eldest, I spoke to her, but her back was toward me and she didn't hear me. "Jesus!" she said again. Horrified, I went in and asked her what the problem was. She held up the baby figurine in the manger and said, "We're going for a ride and he won't get into his car seat!"

▶ OH BROTHER

On the Monday after his Mom delivered a little girl, 5-year-old Tommy returned to kindergarten. "I've got a new baby sister!" he proudly exclaimed to the teacher as he walked into the classroom that morning.

"I heard about that, Tommy," said the teacher. "You must be very excited."

"Yup! But it's the last one," he noted.

"Oh, really?"

"Yup! Mom had her boobs tied."

If it's sanity you're after, there's no recipe like laughter.
Henry Rutherford Elliot

Lighten Up and Laugh

► LOVE AND LAUGHTER

Laughter can be serious business. When Rita was preparing for marriage, she and her fiancé took a course for couples where one of the instructor's comments was, "Laughter in each other's presence is one of the best signs of a healthy relationship." She pulled the presenter aside at the break and admitted that she and her intended did not laugh when they were together. "Oh, just nerves before the big day," she was told. Five years later, when I met her in the shelter, she told me she had never been able to laugh in her husband's presence.

> *Wit is the only wall between us and the dark.*
>
> Mark Van Doren

I once saw a plaque that read, "Know why angels fly? They take themselves lightly." So how do we lighten up? Hang around with funny people. Listen to a comedian's tape. Follow our 'wild hairs' when we get a silly idea. Relax.

One of my favorite fortieth birthday parties was one where each of us was given an assignment from Judith and Richard Wilde's book, *101 Ways to Stay Young*. We had people walking with pop cans on their feet; playing kazoo combs; wearing half dollars as monocles; making fish faces; and wearing napkin bras. And we were all sober.

One of the reasons people consume so much alcohol in America is so we can let our hair down. The goal as we become healthier and happier is to become so self-comfortable that we can do the fun things we used to have to explain under the guise of "I was young then" or "I was drunk."

Recently, in a class I was teaching for recovering addicts, a young man named Pat reminded me that in order to stay sober, we can't be too somber. I had walked in that morning in what I call my "Caribbean dress," and received many "oohs" and "ahs." As I was thanking a woman for her compliment, this strapping Irishman asked, "If I ever decide to cross-dress, can I borrow it?"

Humor is the hole that lets a little sawdust out of a stuffed shirt.

Beware of any event where laughter is not allowed. I have sung at funerals and weddings for years, and find that of the two, weddings are much more up-tight and less prone to a good belly laugh.

This rule was broken recently at a wedding ceremony officiated by a friend of mine. The bride was incredibly nervous despite my friend's repeated attempts to lighten up the affair. Finally, at the end of the ceremony, he broke through her tension as he said,

"And Julie told me no matter what, I couldn't forget this last part: Son, you may kiss the bride!"

Humor is one of my tests of a good friendship. I have a tendency to be unorganized, and it has been amazing to watch the different reactions to my admitted weakness. Back when my corporation was non-profit, our newly hired executive director railed at the board one evening that I was "terribly unorganized!" After a slight pause, one board member pointed out, "If she wasn't, we wouldn't need you, now would we?"

My good friends accept my idiosyncrasies and waste no time teasing me about them. After a concert not long ago, one choir member interrupted a gentleman's praise of my work with, "Yes, she gifted, but don't put her on a pedestal! Next week we're sending her to a class for the Organizationally Impaired!"

I is who I is.
Tom Peterson

When I start to feel down about my weaknesses, I love to remind myself that while Einstein was growing up, he was called 'a moron' by many of his peers. My favorite story took place while he was a passenger on a train.

As the story goes, the conductor walked up to take his ticket and watched as Einstein frantically searched through his pockets for the important item. "Oh, Dr. Einstein," the conductor blurted out, "I didn't realize it was you!" He went on to say what an honor it was to have such a guest aboard his train, as the prestigious passenger continued his desperate search.

"Sir, I don't need your ticket. Sorry to have bothered you," the conductor offered.

"I need my ticket!" Einstein exclaimed. "I don't know where I'm going!"

Seeing the weaknesses of this genius helps me laugh at my own.

1. Do I have any sacred cows where my humanness is concerned that I am unwilling to laugh at?

_____

_____

_____

_____

_____

_____

_____

2. Have I milked them for all they're worth? (get it?)

_____

_____

3. What labels of "_____-challenged" can I give to myself? (e.g., follically challenged for balding, chronologically challenged for aging, etc.)

_____

_____

_____

_____

_____

I know that for every door that closes, another one opens,
but these hallways are the pits!

Refrigerator magnet

 SEX IS NOT A FOUR-LETTER WORD

On a day-to-day basis, the most important key to humor is to just relax. Through humor, we can safely discuss what it's difficult to talk about. That is probably why sex is the focus of so many more jokes than any other topic.

It's so important to feel our feelings.
When I want to cry, I think of my sex life.
When I want to laugh, I think of my sex life.

Glenda Jackson

And then there are sex differences. These are my two favorites:

▷ **TOP 10 REASONS WHY IT'S GREAT TO BE A GUY** ◁

1. Phone conversations are over in 30 seconds flat
2. A 5-day vacation only requires one suitcase
3. You can open all your own jars
4. Your last name stays put
5. The world is your urinal
6. You don't have to remember everybody's birthday
7. One mood, all the time
8. You can whip your shirt off on a hot day
9. Three pairs of shoes are more than enough
10. Chocolate is just another snack

L

Lighten Up and Laugh ☺

And not to leave women out... keep smiling!

 TOP 10 T-SHIRT SLOGANS FOR WOMEN

10. So many men, so few who can afford me.

9. At my age, I've seen it all, done it all, heard it all...I just can't remember it all.

8. If you want breakfast in bed, sleep in the kitchen.

7. Dinner is ready when the smoke alarm goes off.

6. Princess, having had sufficient experience with princes, seeks frog.

5. Warning: I have an attitude and I know how to use it.

4. God made us sisters, Prozac made us friends.

3. All dressed up and no one to choke.

2. Next mood swing, 6 minutes.

1. If we are what we eat, I'm fast, cheap and easy!

So, go read a funny book, or take a funny friend out for pineapple right-side-up cake. Then, consider these suggestions:

♦ Listen to a comedy tape on your way to work.

♦ Post cartoons around your home and office.

♦ Read the funnies.

♦ Have a puppet in your car for traffic jams. Then put on a show for all the other drivers stopped in traffic.

♦ Wear colorful suspenders.

♦ Go to a park and play on the swings and slides.

♦ Give a silly name to a machine you work with or drive.

♦ Tickle someone.

♦ Wear sexy underwear. (Or...???)

♦ Smile. (It changes the chemistry of every cell in your body.)

♦ Buy a desk toy that winds up or pops.

♦ Leave a mysterious message on your co-worker's/supervisor's answering machine.

♦ Have a 'take your child to work' day. Okay, maybe only half a day!

♦ Sing in the shower or at a karaoke bar... but don't quit your day job!

♦ Organize a 'Guess-The-Baby-Pictures' contest for your co-workers.

♦ Have a stress ball handy for when someone needs to squeeze the air out of something! (Drawing someone's face on it is optional!)

♦ Go skinny-dipping or play ice ball, depending on the climate.

♦ Put a goofier than Goofy message on your answering machine.

♦ Every time you hear a good joke, write it down and leave it on three other people's answering machines.

♦ Buy mini M&M's and throw them at unsuspecting passersby.

♦ Stand waiting to greet the garbage collection team with drums, horns, party hats, and a sign that says, "Just a litter message to say **thank you!**"

Life is too important to be taken seriously.

A good friend of mine is a veterinarian who writes wonderfully humorous poetry for when he gives talks to his peers. He shared with me recently that he had a really hard time in college, and the thing that got him through was being chosen to be the class 'Critic' for two out of his four years. This was the student whose job it was to make fun of the programs and professors. He went on to explain, "It absolutely saved me. I couldn't have done it without the perspective that humor offered."

It's even important to laugh at what we've covered in this book. I always know an audience 'got' my message when I hear them mocking me with it as I leave. One of the most sensitive men I know heard me talk about feelings and added his favorite quote about guys...

It really does take a big man to cry,
but it takes an even bigger man to laugh at him.

Jack Handy

 BE LIKE THE LITTLE CHILDREN

If we think about it, to let go of worry and "not sweat the small stuff" is to live the carefree life of a child. Adults average 17 laughs a day; children over 200. No one laughs as often or as long at absolutely nothing as a child. So let us "be like the little children" in this regard. Child-like laughter is good for the soul, the body, and the "never mind."

He who laughs, lasts.

Bumper Snicker

Self Nurturing: ◀ Taking Care of Me One Day at a Time

Compulsively proper and generous people predominate among cancer patients because they put the needs of others in front of their own.

Bernie Siegel, M.D.

Most of this book has been about the big picture, the patterns that form over time that are either helpful or destructive. This chapter, however, isn't about your life per se. It's about feeling joy *today*. I'm going to invite you to do something to take care of yourself and enjoy pleasure in the *next 24 hours*. It's not really important what you choose to do to self-nurture, it is important that you do it. To illustrate, let me describe an evening of mine about a year ago.

I was feeling down. A few months out of a relationship, in the midst of three deadlines, and trying to lose weight so my clothes would fit again, it was a Saturday night.

The kids were at Dad's, my girlfriends and the gang I hang with were out of town for the weekend, and I was new at my church and hadn't really established new friends there, so things were quiet. I decided to run to the store to grab a few things. Driving home, I felt restless. I reviewed my options in my head. With each, I placed a 'value' number.

- Stop at a fast food restaurant and stuff myself with a shake,   -8
  fries and cookies.
- Rent a movie.   +2
- Call old boyfriend to come help me balance my checkbook.   -10
- Put pictures in a scrapbook.   +5
- Call my Mom.   +8

- Come home and clean house.   +10
- Get on the Internet and chat.   -6
- Come home and balance my checkbook myself.   +10
- Come home and take a hot bath and read a book.   +5

So, the decision was obvious, right? Come home, clean house, balance my checkbook and go to bed, right? NOT! First of all, if I have in my head that those are the 'right' choices, anything less brings me guilt. Yet, the chances that I'll get any of that done in the mood I'm in are slim and none. I needed to do something enjoyable, not productive.

▶ #1 Rule of Self Nurturing: You cannot do the great big things until you do the great small things.

I know of way too many folks who never get around to achieving their dreams because they wouldn't take a night off to just kick back and take a break. So what I ended up doing was buying two cookies at a fast food place and savoring both of them while reading one of my favorite books. It was not only a short-term great decision, it was a long-term great decision. Why?

1. I didn't go to bed feeling 'deprived' and then have to make it up by binge eating or goofing off all the next week. (Both of which I have done in the past.)

2. By giving myself permission to take a break from being productive and doing a 'want' instead of a 'should' in my life, I was self-honoring and loving. This energized me the following day, when I did do scrapbooks and checkbooks (without ex-boyfriend help.)

Once I became conscious and nonjudgmental of my needs and my energy levels, here is how I re-rated my options for the evening:

- Stop at a fast food restaurant and buy two cookies.   +7
- Rent a movie.   +6
- Call old boyfriend to come help me balance my checkbook.   -10
- Put pictures in a scrapbook. (not fun for me at the time)   0
- Call my Mom.   +4
  (I did it the following day when I was in a better mood.)
- Come home and clean house.   -9
- Get on an Internet chat.   -8
- Come home and balance my checkbook myself.   -10
- Come home and take a bubble bath and read a book.   +10

Now, on a different day, going and working out or tanning might have been a fun thing to do, or sitting by the fire and roasting marshmallows in the winter. The moral here is that seemingly non-productive choices *will produce* the highest benefit in the long run. Take off your "My Mom would be proud of me" badge and just be what she would call "lazy" for an hour each day. We won't tell her. In fact, she might like a copy of this book! ☺

Note: If your self nurturing time ends up being TV more than one hour a couple of days a week, you're kidding yourself. Spending time watching other people live their lives does not count for you living yours!

To see if you might be one of those who needs to take more time off for fun and self nurturing, take the following inventory:

▶ ARE YOU IN JOY DEBT?

1. Does your lack of joy and fun in your life put a strain on your close relationships?

2. Have you developed a reputation for being too intense or overly serious?

3. Has your lack of self nurturing caused you to resent your job, church or family?

4. Do you find yourself lying about how happy you are and how well things are going?

5. Have you ever sworn that you'll never go this long without a break or a vacation again?

6. Do you endanger your health by going for long periods of time without self nurturing and fun?

7. When invited to a party, do you feel like you won't have or be fun and therefore feel uncomfortable about going?

8. Does your lack of joy ever cause you to binge on things such as spending, food, drink, Internet, sex, gambling or TV?

9. Do you think you can only have fun if you are doing the above? (see #8)

10. Do you tend to schedule yourself for fun experiences, but then find projects at work or home that keep you from allowing yourself to take part in them?

11. Do you justify your lack of joy by telling yourself that it's temporary?

12. Do you justify your lack of joy by convincing yourself and others that no one can do what you're doing and that you are indispensable?

13. Do you tend to analyze your fun experiences, rather than allow yourself to relish them?

14. Do you tend to judge people who are having fun as 'frivolous', 'absurd' or 'empty'?

15. Do you have trouble being around or playing with children?

16. Do you consider going for a walk, going on a picnic or getting together with a friend for coffee or a drink 'a waste of time'?

17. Do you find yourself regularly regretting the fun you did not have earlier in your life, or even yesterday?

18. Do you tend to run around and work hard so that others can have fun, but not have fun yourself?

19. Do you feel envious when you see people out laughing and having fun with friends?

20. Do you tell yourself that after this crisis/school year/project is over, you'll take time to enjoy yourself more?

If you answered YES to 5 or more of the above questions, you are ready to waste some major time!

Your homework is to do the small fun things, one a day, for 15–45 minutes, and you will have more time (trust me on this one) and energy to accomplish your great big fun things.

Need some ideas on Self Nurturing Fun-isms? Here are some examples of ways of taking care of me:

Note: Before you select one of the following to InJoy, HALT!
    Ask yourself if you are Hungry, Angry, Lonely or Tired.
        If you are Hungry, go eat something.
        If you are Angry, go write something.
        If you are Lonely, go call someone.
        If you are Tired, go to sleep.

Once those are taken care of, here are...

▷ **Fun–isms for Taking Care of Me** ◁

- Hug someone
- Hold a baby
- Have a manicure/pedicure/facial
- Read a magazine article
- Smile at remembering the last time you laughed really hard
- Lay on the ground and look up at the stars or clouds
- Take a day off from both work and worry
- Have a good cry
- Write a thank you note
- Take a bubble bath with scented candles
- Go to a really good hair stylist
- Buy a pair of really wild or really comfortable shoes
- Wash your car, inside and out
- Journal 20 things you're grateful for
- Hire it done:
    - Housecleaning
    - Painting
    - Cooking
    - Dog Training
    - Yardwork

- ◆ Errands
- ◆ Organizing
- ◆ Shopping
- ◆ Car Washing
- Set a boundary
- Wear something beautiful/meaningful
- Throw/give stuff away
- Read a love, mystery or sci-fiction novel
- Swing on a swing or slide on a slide
- Take a deep breath
- Say a prayer/meditate
- Buy flowers for your table or desk
- See a counselor
- Go for a walk
- Go out to eat
- Delegate
- Sign up for a fun class
- Get a massage
- Go biking or dancing or rollerblading
- Bake something
- Listen to a motivational/inspirational tape
- Start a support group
- Take a trip/go fishing
- Have your picture taken or painted
- Sing or hum or play the piano or listen to a favorite song
- Take yourself out on a date
- Daydream about your next house/car/job/relationship
- Eat chocolate
- Go to a museum, comedy show or a movie
- Go to a zoo or an arboretum
- Read old love letters or write yourself one
- Read the funnies
- Be

▶Shift Happens: Tools for Transition

"Who are you?" asked the caterpillar...
"I-I hardly know, Sir, just at present," Alice replied rather shyly.
"At least I know who I was when I got up this morning,
but I think I must have changed several times since then."
From Lewis Carroll's *Alice's Adventures in Wonderland*

W ell, has anything changed for you since you started this book? I sincerely hope you've experienced the joy of taking control of your life! This time through the book, I started the habit of writing myself love letters from the chapter on Habit J. It has been transforming!

Well, before I close, here are some thoughts intended to increase your comfort level as you continue along your way...

▶ HOW CHANGE HAPPENS

Some behavioral researchers say it takes 21 days of repeating a new behavior daily to create a habit. Others say 14 days. Still others say it takes 12 months to see real progress. Whatever the amount of time needed to make lasting change, it is neither instant nor eternal. When we are faithful to the goal of health and happiness, 'shift' happens. An important step in making positive changes is to alter how we think about change itself.

I remember the day I ran to my counselor because I was backsliding. I had been free from my pattern of binge-eating for about six months when a week of chaos and crisis hit. I lost my bearings, ate a huge package of potato chips, and sat totally discouraged in his office as I told him of the experience.

"Mary Kay," he shared, "habits are like canyons. You had an old canyon of binge eating behavior; now you've been digging a new canyon of healthy eating habits. You need to realize two things:

"First, your new canyon isn't as deep as your old one. This means that when a problem gets you all turned around, you will still naturally return to the old canyon. Secondly, the dirt from digging the new canyon isn't filling up the old one. The old one will stay with you forever. Your goal is to make the new canyon deeper so that you automatically resort to a healthier set of behaviors."

"How long do I have to wait for the new canyon to be deeper?" I asked.

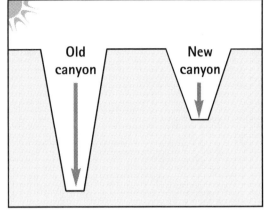

"You've been binge-eating for about seven years, so I'd guess around seven months or so."

I truly appreciated his formula: One month of the new for every year of the old. It helped me to be patient with the process. Often I see people who read a book and believe they are then 'fixed'. We just aren't programmed that way. I have seen miraculous, seemingly overnight turn-arounds, but I know that the new behaviors didn't click in overnight. There were many dark nights of the soul that were encountered along the way before the new lifestyle could stick.

On the lighter side, look at how a toddler becomes potty-trained. At first, he doesn't notice that the 'mess' has happened. He keeps wondering why the living room or the bedroom smells so bad! We, too, sometimes wonder why life 'stinks', overlooking the true source of the problem.

Next, the toddler figures out: "The smell is coming from me!" Once he discovers what behavior is creating the problem, he tries to change overnight. But, oops! Sometimes, it's in the middle of doing things the old way that the moment of awareness occurs. Finally, the little one successfully catches himself before the 'accident' occurs, and changes his behavior.

No one faults a toddler for taking time to make the transition. We can decide to be just as patient with ourselves.

▶ MEASURING THE MAGNITUDE OF CHANGE

There are three ways to go about change. For some, like me, the all-at-once dramatic change works best. For others, it's more helpful to start small. So let's look at the advantages of each size of change.

For our purposes, I'll use the analogy of shedding our skin to describe the size of changes we can make.

1. The lobster way is dramatic and complete

2. The snake way is more gradual, in layers

3. The human way is constant and in very small increments

► The Lobster

The lobster, like many of us, resists change. It builds a wall around itself in the form of a hard shell, and only changes when its 'inner growth' causes too much pain to tolerate. Once the lobster outgrows its shell, however, huge, dramatic change is no longer merely a choice, it is the only means of survival. The lobster will suffocate if it does not change. Thus, the creature cracks its shell and crawls out, leaving all of its safety behind until it grows a new shell.

I have seen men and women who have gone through similar dramatic changes in their lives. Their pain is so intense that they release what seems the whole of their old beliefs and behaviors in one fell swoop.

I'll always remember the attractive woman in her 30's who yelled out "Yes!" at the end of her first two-hour class with me. Four classes later, she shared with us that she quit drinking and smoking and kicked out her abusive boyfriend that first evening. (I saw her a year and a half later and all three changes were still in place!)

While this dramatic, instantaneous change is exhilarating, there is great chance of relapse due to one's vulnerability. As with the lobster, it takes a long time for the new 'self' to become solid. We learn quickly to care less about what others think, because this kind of change attracts attention ("You used to be such fun!") and we have to get used to dealing with it.

The good news is that, just as the lobster's new shell is larger, these individuals also move into a new, more expansive consciousness that benefits them for life. The larger changes, because they include new boundaries and have fairly immediate, dramatic results, are more difficult at first. But they are usually fairly easy to maintain. To go back to our old selves, once we've made the leap, would cause a lot of unwanted attention to come our way!

> *Change is not made without inconvenience,*
> *even from worse to better.*
>
> Samuel Johnson

In changing my diet to more low-fat choices, I learned a lot from the book/tape by Dr. Dean Ornish called, *Eat More, Weigh Less.* He states "Comprehensive changes are easier to sustain than moderate ones." For example, because of the immediate rewards, it's easier to stop eating red meat altogether than to cut down. Often we feel better, more energized immediately. As Ornish states, "Joy is a much more powerful motivator than fear."

► The Snake

The snake chooses a less exciting approach to change, shedding his skin in layers. He waits until a summer's day when the heat becomes uncomfortable and then slides out, releasing one coat of skin at a time.

When we have put off making changes in our lives, this shedding becomes necessary. For one individual, it might be asking for a much-deserved raise: for another, asking a roommate to smoke outside. These changes are not usually earth shattering, but they can definitely increase our heart rates as we go through a time of transition.

I recently talked to parents of a teen-ager complaining about having trouble with their son. Upon inquiry, I discovered they were still using the "because I said so," response to his questions. This technique is fine for four and five year olds who can't understand all the 'whys' of rules and discipline, but it's inappropriate for older children. Once we practiced some new ways of listening and sharing, the parents were willing to shed old behaviors for a newer, fresher approach. Although uncomfortable at first, these moderate transitions can yield very encouraging results.

► The Human

Finally, there is the way you and I shed every cell of our skin every year. This process is so natural to us that we are not even conscious that it is happening. Yet none of our skin cells are more than twelve months old!

Lived out, this pattern would be embodied by people who are comfortable with change, who 'go with the flow' more easily than their peers. They non-aggressively speak their opinions on a regular basis. When change doesn't find them, they look for change.

A good example of this is someone who reads publications to keep up on the latest news in their interest area, or someone who continues to challenge themselves physically by jet-skiing one year, running a half-marathon the next, and sky-diving the next. People who are comfortable with change tend to enjoy travel because it continues to stretch them and help them grow.

With this attitude toward change, there are fewer big risks needed because of the smaller ones taken along the way. If we put off change, we face having to 'shed' everything at once. Then we feel naked, as I did years ago when leaving my marriage and beliefs about myself behind. If, on the other hand, we allow the sometimes-painful truths of life to transform us on a daily basis, and stay open to new ways of thinking and acting, our soaring to new heights will be a lot smoother.

If you could accept that you are a magnificent, worthy,
lovely, perfect, creative being and that all is well,
you would be a long way towards living your dreams.

Abraham-Hicks

I once shared with a friend that I had veered 'off my path' and she reminded me that that was impossible. Wherever I am today *is* my path, and I need to release any picture or expectation of what my recovery and enlightenment process will look like.

I promise you, friend, that once you and I change our minds, the behavioral changes will come. There will be some pain and anxiety along the way, but there is no match for the rewards that await heroes like us at the end of our journey.

Death to the caterpillar,
to the butterfly is being set free.

►In Conclusion

At the end of his initial consultation with each patient,
the famous psychoanalyst Alfred Adler would ask a powerful question:
"And what would you do if you were cured?"
After his client answered, Adler would respond,
"Then go and do it!"

All of life's problems originate within, either from:

- Judgment of self and others
- Despair, or
- Fear

With that understanding, the keys to happiness are clear:

- Forgiveness
- Gratitude, and
- Hope

I grew up hearing about love and happiness from family and church, and was frustrated that I had no formula for either. Now I know that the formula is composed of the simple behaviors we have discussed here.

These lessons are not new. They have been passed down through the ages for each generation, each individual to rediscover and express. We cannot do otherwise. Even on our darkest days we are learning the lessons of love and happiness. We are right where we're supposed to be, today, this moment. Life and learning are the great adventures. Love and happiness are the great rewards.

The truest measurement of your success is not in outward manifestations...
it is in how you are feeling right now.

Abraham-Hicks

I am in true gratitude for this rewriting. It has been cathartic in ways I could not have imagined. Just when I needed to focus on a particular subject, that was the chapter I was working on that day! It has reminded me, as I hope it has you, that we do not need to create happiness. It is within us each moment, longing for expression. Happiness is our destiny. All we need do is return to it.

Welcome Home.

Index of Quotes◄

Index/Bibliography ◀

Following each index entry are listed books (B) on that subject which are recommended by the author for further reading and films (F) which are relevant to the subject. InJoy!